HOW TO REDUCE THE TAX YOU PAY

Planning

HOW TO

through 1999,

REDUCE

plus tips

THE TAX

for 1998 returns

YOU PAY

KEY PORTER BOOKS

Canadian Cataloguing in Publication Data
The National Library of Canada has catalogued this publication as follows:
Main entry under title:
How to reduce the tax you pay
Annual.
[1988] –
ISSN 1187-0028
ISBN 1-55263-044-7 (1998: Deloitte & Touche)
ISBN 1-55263-056-0 (1998: Samson Bélair/Deloitte & Touche)
1. Tax Planning—Canada—Periodicals. 2. Income tax—Canada—Periodicals. Deloitte & Touche. II. Samson Bélair/Deloitte & Touche (Firm)
HJ4661.H68   343.7105'2'05   C94-090997-0

Key Porter Books Limited
70 The Esplanade
Toronto, Ontario
Canada M5E 1R2

www.keyporter.com

Electronic formatting: Heidi Palfrey

Printed and bound in Canada

98 99 00 01 6 5 4 3 2 1

....

Acknowledgments

How to Reduce the Tax You Pay was compiled by a team of writers from Deloitte & Touche LLP and (in Quebec) Samson Bélair/Deloitte & Touche.

Deloitte & Touche LLP is one of Canada's leading professional services firms, providing accounting, tax, financial, business advisory and consulting services to Canadian clients since 1858. The firm has more than 4,500 people, including more than 550 partners, serving corporate, owner-managed, not-for-profit and public sector organizations, as well as individual clients, from 56 offices across the country.

Deloitte & Touche LLP is part of Deloitte Touche Tohmatsu, one of the world's largest providers of accounting, tax and professional services, with more than 72,000 people in 127 countries.

EXECUTIVE EDITORS

Paul Alliston, Toronto
Richard Wilson, Montreal

PRODUCTION EDITORS

Gisèle Archambault, Montreal
Bill Sherman, Toronto

CONTRIBUTORS

Alan Arsenault, Calgary
Mario Bastonnais, Montreal
Marty Blatt, Edmonton
John Bowey, Kitchener
Peter Clayden, Vancouver
Charles Evans, Kitchener
Heather Evans, Toronto
Sharon Forsey, St. John's
Daryl Hanstke, Kitchener
Steve Henderson, Vancouver
René Huot, Montreal
John Hutson, Kitchener
Brian Janzen, Winnipeg
Anne Montgomery, Toronto

Sandra Pearson, Toronto
Keith Pitzel, Winnipeg
Len Sakamoto, Toronto
Nick Seed, Toronto
Karen Slezak, Toronto
Brian Taylor, Saskatoon

CONTRIBUTING EDITOR

Marisha Roman, Toronto

PRODUCTION SUPPORT

Junia Fulgence, Toronto

DISCLAIMER

The information and analysis contained in this book are not intended to substitute for competent professional advice. Planning your tax and financial affairs to reduce the tax you pay is a complex process—one that is unique to you or your business. The material that follows is provided solely as a general guide to assist you in understanding the main income tax provisions you can use to minimize your tax burden. No action should be initiated without consulting your professional advisors. This book reflects the law and legislative proposals to October 1, 1998.

Contents

How to Use This Book

Do you want to pay more income tax than the law requires?

Of course you don't—but that is exactly what many Canadians do. Some may fail to understand the tax rules and amendments, or how they are applied. Others miss out on tax planning opportunities that the law provides, or fail to take advantage of specific tax incentives that are readily available. Far too many taxpayers make errors in completing their tax returns, errors that the tax department may not be able to identify or correct. And finally, some people just can't seem to meet the deadlines imposed under the law, and therefore end up paying interest and penalties on top of what they owe.

We think this book can help you to avoid costly mistakes, and to reduce or defer your tax burden through intelligent planning—both for your 1998 return and throughout 1999.

NEW TO THIS EDITION

This 11th edition continues the revised format that we introduced a year ago. Our "New for 1998!" sections keep you up to date on the latest tax changes affecting the 1998 tax year. Look for significant changes in the tax benefits and credits for individuals with children and those who provide care for elderly parents. Look also for information on how you can use your RRSP investments to fund a return to school in Chapter 14. In addition, we have added essential tax filing information for our readers who hold offshore investments. Read Chapter 10 to get the most recent information on the reporting changes for foreign investment property, which will be in effect for the 1998 tax year.

If you are looking for a "big-picture" view of the taxation of income in Canada, we invite you to read this guide from cover to cover. If, on the other hand, you are looking for information specific to your situation, you can quickly access the most up-to-date data in the chapter or section relating to your situation.

Tax Calendar[1]

December 31, 1998	Due date for single instalment of 1998 taxes for farmers and fishermen.
February 28, 1999	Last day for filing 1998 T4 and T5 summaries and sending slips to payees.
March 1, 1999	Last day for RRSP contributions eligible for deduction from 1998 personal income tax.
March 15, 1999	Due date for 1st quarterly instalment of 1999 personal income taxes.
April 15, 1999	Due date for 1998 U.S. personal income tax returns and last day for filing for extension.
April 30, 1999	Due date for filing 1998 personal income tax returns and for payment of balance of 1998 income taxes. Where a taxpayer died in 1998, terminal return due on the later of April 30, 1999, or six months following the date of death.
June 15, 1999	Due date for 2nd quarterly instalment of 1999 personal income taxes.
September 15, 1999	Due date for 3rd quarterly instalment of 1999 personal income taxes.
November 1999	Good month for taking a final look at your tax planning for 1999.
December 15, 1999	Due date for 4th quarterly instalment of 1999 personal income taxes.
December 31, 1999	Due date for single instalment of 1999 taxes for farmers and fishermen.

[1] Remittances of amounts deducted or withheld are considered to be received on the date they are actually received and not the date they were mailed. Note that if the payments are made at a chartered bank, they are considered to have been received by Revenue Canada at that time.

Tax Planning—Getting Started

WHY PLAN YOUR TAX?

You have answered that question to some extent by buying this book. No one, including you, should pay more tax than the law requires. The best way of ensuring that you pay only your fair share of taxes is through tax planning. Don't mistake effective tax planning with tax evasion. Tax evasion is any manoeuvre undertaken to hide income otherwise subject to tax; for example, failing to declare all your interest income on your tax return. Tax planning, on the other hand, involves reviewing your financial goals, and arranging your activities to achieve those goals in the most tax-effective manner by using tax rules that permit you to reduce or defer taxation, increase deductions, or avoid tax traps.

Tax "Loopholes"

Most people assume that you can save your tax dollars only through loopholes, those inadvertent errors in the design and structure of the *Income Tax Act*. In fact, tax incentives have been specially implemented by law in our *Income Tax Act* to encourage certain tax-planned activities. If you take advantage of these incentives, you are doing precisely what the government encourages you and other taxpayers to do. These provisions, most of which we cover in this book, are therefore the exact opposite of loopholes.

Time Value of Money

Tax planning, and the resulting tax savings, will help you to optimize the time value of your money. The essence of this concept is that one dollar received today is worth more to us than the same dollar received in the future. For example, if we receive one dollar today, we can invest it to earn interest. After one year, we will have one dollar plus the interest income. If we do not receive that dollar until the end of the year, we have lost the opportunity to earn the interest. Similarly, paying one dollar in taxes today is more expensive than doing so in the future because we lose the interest that dollar could have earned.

WHERE TO BEGIN

Usually, the first step in effective tax planning is to find out where you stand today. Chapter 20 contains statistical tables to help you to determine your tax position for 1998. Use these tables to calculate your approximate tax liability for this year. Refer back to these tables after reading the various strategies explained in this book to determine your potential tax savings.

Setting Your Goals

Your primary tax objective should be to ensure that the taxable income you earn is recognized at a time, and in a form, in which it will be most favourably taxed. There are limits to the benefits of tax planning, however.

Caution: A particular tax incentive or tax plan cannot convert a bad investment into a good one.

Suppose an investment generates tax deductions of $100, resulting in a real tax saving of about $51 for taxpayers in the top bracket. If you anticipate losing the full amount you invested, your real economic cost, after the tax saving, is 49 per cent of the cost. This is not smart tax planning, nor is it a "tax shelter." This is a foolish investment!

The process of setting tax-saving goals requires that you understand the basic concepts of how income is taxed in Canada. We'll discuss these in the next chapter. Other factors to consider in your planning include current interest rates, projected inflation rates, current income tax rules, and the possibility of future legislative changes. After referring to this guide, put your tax plans on paper and then sit down with your spouse and/or children. Discuss your family finances and tax plans together in such a way that everybody can understand your objectives. Open discussion will both encourage and educate your family about financial and tax planning—important lifetime lessons. Once you have considered all the factors relevant to your situation, you and your family can implement your tax plan.

GETTING STARTED

In spite of all the hoopla, tax planning is essentially a simple process with a few basic elements. Because it is a year-round activity, it should be an integral part of your regular financial planning and budgeting process. Unless you have planned carefully throughout the year, opportunities for reducing your tax bill become more and more restricted as the end of the year approaches. Tax planning is most effective if begun immediately.

Get started!

Tax Planning for Today— The Basic Concepts

In order to plan effectively, you should understand the underlying principles of how we are taxed in Canada, how government-legislated tax incentives work, and finally, how to choose which tax strategy is best suited to you. In this chapter, we look at how income is taxed in Canada.

THE CONCEPT OF INCOME

Since you are taxed differently depending on the type of income you earn, the first step in tax planning is to identify your sources of income. There are three main categories of taxable income: employment income, business income, and income from property and capital gains. There are also forms of income that are not taxable, but for the most part, if you have received a benefit of any kind from any activity, it is likely to be taxable.

THE THREE BASIC TYPES OF INCOME

Employment Income

Most Canadians earn the bulk of their income through employment. Employment income includes all benefits you receive in connection with the services you provide to your employer. Your employer will withhold and remit on your behalf your income tax and other payments to Revenue Canada. You are responsible for including the T4s issued by your employer when filing your annual tax return.

Business Income

If you earn income from a business activity, your taxable income will be derived from the "profits" of the business. Profits are calculated by subtracting the expenses incurred in generating earned revenue from the earned revenue. If you realize a loss on the activity, this loss may offset income from other sources, including employment and investment income. The deductibility of farming losses from other sources of income is restricted.

If the revenue-generating activity gives rise to income from the disposition of property, the income either will be fully included in calculating taxable income or will be a capital gain, eligible for a partial exclusion. The determination of this issue depends on the nature of your business. For example, if your business revolves around the buying and selling of real estate, income earned from any disposition of property will likely be income from a business.

Property Income and Capital Gains

The third major income category is income from property, including interest, dividends, and rent. Capital gains are connected with property income, but are subject to special rules for the taxable amounts. We'll talk further about these in Chapter 9.

Gains from transfers of property (sales, gifts, etc.), including gains from sales of property used solely for personal purposes, are generally taxable. The primary exceptions to this rule are certain tax-deferred transfers between spouses, certain transfers of farm property to children, and gains from the sale of a personal residence if it is designated as your principal residence.

OTHER INCOME

Most income from sources other than employment, business, or property is probably taxable. While we cannot cover all of the possibilities in this book, here are some of the more common alternative sources of income for Canadians. If you are in doubt, seek professional advice.

Alimony and Maintenance Payments

Discussed further in Chapter 12.

Child Support Payments

Discussed further in Chapter 12.

Annuities

An annuity is an agreement for periodic payments over a specified period of time. It may be purchased with after-tax or before-tax dollars. For example, if you invest RRSP assets in an annuity contract, you are using before-tax dollars. On the other hand, if you use your savings to buy an annuity contract, you will be using after-tax dollars. The nature of the income used to purchase the annuity determines whether income earned from the annuity will be taxable.

If an annuity payment is received from a contract purchased through a tax-exempt fund or plan, the full amount of the payment is taxable as income in the year you receive it. Most common examples of such annuity payments include amounts from pension plans and RRSPs. See also Chapter 14 for a discussion of RRSP annuities.

If you have purchased the annuity with after-tax funds, a portion of each payment under the contract is excluded from your taxable income. The portion is calculated using your original investment in the contract, which has already been taxed.

EXEMPT INCOME

A surprising fact for many Canadians is that it is possible to receive income that is not taxable at all. The following are two of the more common examples.

Gifts and Inheritances

A gift or inheritance is not taxed as income to the person receiving the property. The individual making the gift is considered, with certain exceptions such as spousal transfers, to have sold the property at its fair market value on the date of transfer by Revenue Canada. As a result, the individual making the gift will accrue taxable income on any realized capital gains, while the recipient will be treated as having acquired the property at the fair market value on the date of transfer. If the recipient sells or transfers the property at a future date, any capital gain realized at that time will be calculated from the original date of the gift.

Lotteries, Gambling, and Other Prize Winnings

Gains resulting from games of chance (e.g., lotteries and gambling) are not included in income. If you receive prizes related to your employment, however, they are likely to be considered connected with services rendered and therefore taxable as employment income.

CANADA'S GRADUATED TAX SYSTEM

Marginal Tax Brackets

Canada's personal income tax system was originally designed with a built-in fairness system in the form of graduated rates of tax. As your taxable income increases, the percentage of tax that must be paid on that income also increases. In other words, income that falls into a higher tax bracket is more heavily taxed than income that falls into a lower tax bracket. Different tax rates at different income levels result in marginal tax brackets, which tell us how much will be paid to the government in taxes from each additional dollar of taxable income we earn.

Understanding the concept of marginal tax brackets is essential for successful family income planning, in particular income splitting. For example, if the primary earner in the family is in a 45 per cent tax bracket and can transfer income to a family member in a 26 per cent bracket, the family will save 19 cents for every dollar of taxable income transferred (until that family member moves into the next tax bracket).

The marginal tax brackets also tell us how much we will save if we incur costs that are tax-deductible. If your marginal tax bracket is 45 per cent and you can deduct one dollar from that taxable income, you will save 45 cents in taxes; this 45-cent saving means that the actual after-tax cost of spending that tax-deductible dollar is 55 cents. Because of the marginal tax brackets, tax-deductible expenditures are more valuable to high-income taxpayers than to low-income taxpayers.

CHAPTER THREE

The Six Faces of Tax Planning

THE KEY PLANNING CONCEPTS

Tax planning can be broken down into six main strategies:

- *income splitting*—transferring income from a taxpayer in a high tax bracket to one in a lower tax bracket;
- *income shifting*—transferring income from a high-tax-rate year to a lower-rate year; or shifting deductions from a low-rate year to a high-rate year;
- *investment selection*—transforming income from a fully taxed source to one that is eligible for full or partial exemption;
- *tax deferral*—delaying taxation of income;
- *income deferral*—deferring the recognition of income for tax purposes to future years;
- *tax shelters*—using tax law incentives to maximize deductions and minimize taxable income.

Income Splitting

Income splitting occurs when income that normally would be taxed entirely in your hands is taxed in the hands of both you and another person with a lower marginal tax rate, for example, your spouse (including a common-law spouse) or children. If the difference in marginal tax rates is 20 per cent, the family's tax saving is $200 for every $1,000 of income transferred to the lower-rate individual. Successful income splitting also requires that the income transferred does not bump the lower-rate individual to a higher tax rate and that the attribution rules are observed.

The Attribution Rules Defined. The government is aware of the benefits of income splitting and the *Income Tax Act* contains provisions, called the attribution rules, that are designed to discourage income splitting. If a provision of the *Income Tax Act* is contravened because of a transfer of taxable income and the attribution rules are applied, the transferred income will be attributed back to the taxpayer who made the transfer. The transferring taxpayer will then be taxed on the income, despite the fact that the transferring taxpayer did not personally receive it.

Getting Around the Attribution Rules. Generally, because of the breadth of the attribution rules, it has become difficult, if not impossible, to have large amounts of income taxed in your spouse's or children's hands rather than in your hands over a short period of time. For that reason, it is important to begin your income splitting program as early as possible and continually update it to take advantage of the opportunities that remain. Refer to the various planning options discussed in Chapters 11 and 12, but remember that these strategies operate under the assumption that you have and will continue to have a higher tax rate than your spouse and children.

Income Shifting

To gain a tax advantage through income shifting, you must have some idea of your current and future income and be aware of opportunities for controlling the timing of your income flow. Business owners and people working in the professions have more opportunities to shift income than do most employees.

Investment Selection

This strategy requires knowledge of how the different types of income are taxed in Canada. For example, dividends received from Canadian corporations and capital gains are treated more favourably from a tax perspective than interest income. Consequently, from a tax perspective and if returns on investment are equal, investing in Canadian dividend-earning equities is more tax efficient than investing in an interest-earning investment, such as a bond. While this strategy is relatively easy to implement for future investments, before you divest yourself of your interest-earning investments, you should account for any costs you will incur in shifting your investments. For example, you may have to pay a penalty to transfer an investment from an interest-bearing account to one that will provide income in the form of capital gains. If the penalty outweighs the tax benefit, you are well-advised to seek other options.

Tax Deferral

Postponing the payment of taxes is tax deferral. The longer we are able to do so, the longer our money remains available for investment and other activities. The concept of the time value of money plays a significant role. By postponing the payment of taxes, you can take advantage of current investment opportunities.

Income Deferral

Income deferral simply means deferring the recognition of income for tax purposes to future years. The benefit of income deferral is that the payment of tax on that income is postponed. It is sometimes said that tax deferred is tax saved. If, for example, you can defer $1,000 of tax payable for one year, and earn 10 per cent during that time, you have "saved" $100 (less, of course, any tax payable on that $100 of income).

Over the past few years, there has been a significant reduction in the number of opportunities available to defer income, especially with respect to interest income, which must be reported annually even if it has not yet been received (see Chapter 9). These rules affect all taxpayers, including individuals and trusts with individuals as beneficiaries. Income earned in deferred income plans, including registered retirement savings plans, deferred profit sharing plans and registered pension plans, is not affected by these rules, however.

Tax Shelters

Many upper-income Canadians have discovered the hard way that the "quality of the investment" in the tax shelter is by far the most important element, overshadowing all other considerations, including immediate tax savings. Receiving a deduction for the money you put into a tax shelter is no consolation if you end up losing your money because the investment is of poor quality. If you are considering investing in a tax shelter, you should obtain professional advice before committing your funds and future state of mind to these high-risk investments.

CHAPTER FOUR

Tax Planning with the Long View—Estate Planning

Much of this book focuses on how you can save tax dollars today. The fact that you can implement some fairly simple plans to save money in the short term leads us to the next obvious question: What do you do with your money in the future? Retirement and estate planning also raise many taxation issues. Although you might be inclined to skip this chapter, you are mistaken if you believe that you are neither old enough nor rich enough to have an "estate" that is worth planning. Virtually everyone over the age of majority should think about what will happen to his or her assets in the event of death, and should make arrangements to ensure that financially dependent family members are adequately provided for.

> ⚠ **Caution:** Each year, thousands of Canadians die in accidents, and a large number of them die without having made a will. Although the odds are that you will live to a ripe old age, you owe it to yourself, and to your family, to "put your house in order."

Estate planning is the ongoing process of creating and maintaining a program designed to preserve your accumulated wealth and ensure that it is distributed to succeeding generations efficiently and in accordance with your wishes.

Several developments in recent years have affected virtually all existing estate plans and those who are contemplating an estate planning program:

- The abolition of the $100,000 lifetime capital gains exemption in 1994 altered the taxation of assets passed on to succeeding generations.
- The constant tightening of the rules limiting income splitting among family members can necessitate the restructuring of many estate planning approaches.
- The Alternative Minimum Tax affects a number of upper-income Canadians, particularly those with "tax shelter"-type investments.
- New or revised family law legislation in several provinces affects the transfer of assets from one generation to the next.

For residents of Quebec, specific changes to the law of succession were made to the new Civil Code, effective in 1994.

OBJECTIVES

In general, the objectives of effective estate planning are to:

- ensure that you and your family are provided for adequately now and in the future, and that your heirs are adequately provided for after your death;
- distribute assets according to your wishes, both during your lifetime and on your death, with a view to ensuring that the maximum benefits available accrue to your beneficiaries;
- minimize various forms of wealth erosion, with taxes figuring prominently, both now and in the future.

Your estate planning objectives should be realistic. More importantly, your estate plan should be reviewed frequently and be flexible enough to accommodate unexpected changes in your financial or personal situation, as well as changes beyond your control, such as new legislative developments.

Financial Considerations

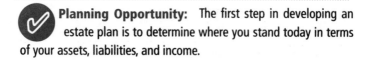

Planning Opportunity: The first step in developing an estate plan is to determine where you stand today in terms of your assets, liabilities, and income.

You should try to create projections for the future direction of your affairs, including possible inheritances, asset liquidations such as the sale of a business or property, the paying off of mortgages, education costs for children, and the acquisition of a recreation or retirement property. At the same time, you should attempt to assess how the economy's performance might affect your assets and income in the future. Use the "rule of 72." For example, if inflation averages 6 per cent a year, one dollar today will be worth 50 cents in today's dollars in approximately 12 years (i.e., 72 divided by 6) and be worth 25 cents in 24 years. If the rate of inflation is 4 per cent, the same result will occur in 18 and 36 years, respectively.

How to Prepare for Meeting with Your Estate Planning Advisor

A professional estate planner needs accurate and up-to-date information concerning your financial affairs, as well as a clear understanding of your financial and personal objectives. He or she must be as well informed about your financial affairs as you are. Once you have selected the estate professional who will manage your estate plan, most often a lawyer (notary in Quebec), ensure that you provide comprehensive information about your finances and future plans. This includes providing lists of your assets and heirs, mortgage documents, RRSP forms, pre-nuptial contracts, and candidates to be your executor(s), among others.

An effective estate plan requires the cooperation and input of a number of individuals, including your accountant, lawyer, insurance agent, financial advisor, and to some extent your business associates. As with your overall tax plan, you should involve your spouse in setting your estate planning objectives. If your affairs are at all complicated and your spouse is expected to manage them upon your death as an executor, involving him or her now makes good sense.

Planning Objectives

From a tax point of view, your estate planning objectives should be to:

- Minimize and defer taxes now and in the future, to preserve your accumulated wealth.
- Shift any potential tax burden associated with a particular asset to your heirs so that taxes become payable only when your heirs eventually dispose of the asset.
- Minimize taxes at death so that as much as possible of your accumulated wealth passes to your heirs.

YOUR CHANGING ESTATE PLAN

Your approach to planning for your estate will change through the various stages of your life. Because your own estate plan will depend on your particular circumstances and those of your family, we can only outline general considerations. The following are intended as descriptions of typical family situations.

Estate Planning Early in Life

During the period from your mid-twenties to about age 40, you will likely have a spouse and start a family, will have little in the way of substantial assets, and will be establishing yourself in your career or business. In this case, your goal is to protect your dependants in the event that you or your spouse should die, or otherwise become unable to provide for them.

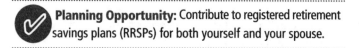

Planning Opportunity: Your estate plan may extend no further than paying down the mortgage on the family home and ensuring that you have sufficient life insurance (likely term insurance) and long-term disability insurance in place.

At this stage, it is likely that, in your will, you would leave all your assets outright to your spouse.

Once you have more income, you will want to start saving for future acquisitions, for your children's education, and for your retirement. This will also affect your estate plan.

Planning Opportunity: Contribute to registered retirement savings plans (RRSPs) for both yourself and your spouse.

At some point, you may find it advantageous to pay higher premiums to obtain the added security and investment benefits available with permanent life insurance.

Planning in Middle Age

From your forties to your mid-fifties, you may well have more substantial assets as a result of a larger family income. However, you may also be facing increased expenditures, such as post-secondary education for your children.

> ✅ **Planning Opportunity:** During this period, continue contributing to a retirement plan, whether an RRSP or a registered pension plan. You may feel you can discontinue your term life insurance policy, while continuing with coverage under a permanent policy.

This also may be a good time to restructure your business affairs and investments to reduce current taxes and facilitate the accumulation of savings and other assets for your retirement.

Pre-Retirement Planning

Once you have reached your mid-fifties, it is time to give serious consideration to planning for your retirement, if you have not already done so.

> ⚠ **Caution:** You must ensure that you secure sufficient retirement income to cover your needs as well as sufficient savings to cover unforeseen events in the near future.

You should continue with contributions to your RRSPs or pension plan, and you will probably continue to make additional investments. You might want to determine what type of retirement income will best suit your needs once your RRSPs and pension plans have matured. If you have a business, you may wish to sell it to further supplement your retirement income, or to pass the management of it to others.

> ⚠ **Caution:** It is important that you keep your will up to date with your family's situation as well as the legislation. Ensure that you have a succession plan if you are a business owner.

The deemed disposition rules in the *Income Tax Act*, which impose a tax on unrealized capital gains at the time of your death, could seriously erode the value of your assets. However, you may be able to minimize the tax consequences of the deemed disposition rules through the careful disposition of your assets during your lifetime and with a carefully drafted will. You may want to consider gifting some of your assets to your heirs during your lifetime, or establishing trusts for their benefit to take effect either during your lifetime or after your death.

YOUR WILL

With regard to creating your own will, you are the testator, if you are a man, or the testatrix, if you are a woman. In your will, you appoint the executor(s) of your estate, name your beneficiaries, and create a distribution plan for your assets. It is important that you consult your spouse in the preparation of your will so that he or she understands the reasons for the provisions that are included. If your spouse does not agree with the terms of the will, provincial family law statutes allow a spouse to challenge a will. This is an expensive and protracted procedure that you should try to avoid wherever possible. Communicating your wishes to your spouse beforehand can prevent such a challenge.

Choosing the Executor

The role of the executor under a will involves onerous responsibilities. You should consider not only the willingness of the person to serve, but also his or her appropriateness for the position. Two of the major criteria are the familiarity of the person with your affairs and the technical competence required to manage your affairs.

> **Caution:** The executor is charged with interpreting your wishes as expressed in your will and in other documents, and carrying them out to the best of his or her ability. Ensure that your will provides clear instructions.

The executor should be empowered by the provisions of your will to make virtually all decisions concerning your estate that you have not anticipated.

Most importantly, your executor is charged with maintaining the value of your estate until assets are distributed to the beneficiaries. This means that if he or she feels your business would benefit from outside management help before your beneficiaries take it over, your will must empower him or her to undertake this arrangement. If these powers are not conferred, and your spouse or your children are incapable of managing the business once they gain control, there is little the executor can do but advise them to bring in outside expertise, or perhaps advise them to sell the business before its value seriously declines.

Understand that a great deal of what happens after your death depends on the arrangements you have made before you die. If your instructions are not specific enough, your executor, although acting in good faith, may misinterpret your wishes or may have his or her powers contested in court.

Dying Intestate

 Caution: In the absence of a will, the distribution of property is determined by provincial laws relating to intestate succession and family law.

Such laws vary from province to province. For example, the law in several provinces provides that if a person dies without a will, a reserve must be set aside for the surviving spouse. The spouse receives an amount equal to the reserve and shares the balance with the children, if any. Since this type of distribution is arbitrary, in most circumstances it will not satisfy the wishes of the deceased and the needs of individual family members.

Reviewing Your Will

A good rule of thumb is that your will should be reviewed, and revised if necessary, at least every five years. Your will should be revised immediately in the event of the death of an intended beneficiary or the executor, or because of changes in your family situation or financial circumstances. Quebec's Civil Code is another reason Quebec residents should have a professional review and, if necessary, modify their will.

Changes in the law may also affect the validity of your will. For instance, in some provinces, legislation respecting division of matrimonial property will override the provisions of your will. This is the case in Quebec with the family patrimony. Furthermore, legislation in most provinces (not including Quebec) provides that you may not totally disinherit your spouse or a dependant. Do not forget to have all the other parts of your estate plan reviewed, such as insurance policies and retirement savings and pension plans. You must remember to change beneficiary designations, or a substantial part of your estate may go to someone you may no longer wish to benefit.

To avoid pitfalls and difficulties in the future, professional legal advice should be sought in all cases from lawyers (notaries in Quebec) experienced in wills and family law. You should also have your tax advisor review the will before you sign it.

TAXATION ON DEATH

If you understand how taxation applies on death, you will be better equipped to decide how to provide effectively for the distribution of your assets in your will, and how to distribute assets during your lifetime, if that is your choice.

There are no Canadian death taxes (estate taxes), federal or provincial, levied on the value of the assets that pass to beneficiaries. Only income amounts received (or deemed to be received) by the deceased and capital gains realized (or deemed to be realized) are subject to income tax.

Upon the death of the testator or testatrix, four distinct taxpaying entities may result: the deceased, the estate (as long as it has not been settled by the executor), any ongoing trusts created under the deceased's will, and finally, the beneficiaries.

Deemed Disposition Rules

In the year of death, an individual's taxation year runs from January 1 to the date of death. A final return of income, the "terminal return," must be filed. The terminal return must report all income earned from January 1 of the year of death to the date of death. Income includes interest, rents, royalties, annuities, remuneration from employment, and other amounts payable on a periodic basis that were accrued but not due at the time of death, as well as amounts due but not paid. Also included are net taxable capital gains or losses realized prior to death and not included in income in a previous year.

In addition to actual earned or realized income, the *Income Tax Act* contains provisions that create deemed income, which must be reported as income in the terminal return. Specifically, the deceased is deemed to have disposed of all capital property immediately before death for consideration equal to its fair market value immediately before death. These deemed dispositions can result in capital gains and losses, as well as a terminal loss or recapture of depreciation already claimed, which must be included in the terminal tax return. "Recapture of depreciation" relates to capital property used to earn income. Taxpayers are entitled to claim a capital cost allowance (CCA) to offset the cost of such capital property against the income earned through the use of the property. The *Income Tax Act* contains regulations that determine the CCA rates. If you sell or transfer capital property for a price greater than its depreciated value, you must account for that gain by including the excess amount as income (a recapture).

A large tax assessment on the "profit" from these deemed dispositions may result. Since there has been no actual sale of assets, the estate may have difficulty paying any taxes that are levied. It should be noted that the Alternative Minimum Tax is not applicable in the year of death.

> **Planning Opportunity:** An individual may avoid some of the adverse tax consequences of the deemed disposition rules by transferring property to a spouse or spousal trust and by transferring any farm property or an interest in a farm property to children.

If property of any kind is transferred to a spouse or spousal trust, no capital gains, recapture of depreciation, etc., arise on death, unless an election is made to claim such income. The spouse or spousal trust inherits the deceased's tax cost (i.e., the cost at which the deceased acquired or was deemed to have acquired the property). Before using this method of relieving taxes, ensure that if the $500,000 lifetime capital gains exemption can apply to the property, it is used. When a principal residence is transferred to a spouse or spousal trust, the spouse or spousal trust retains the deceased's principal residence exemption.

If farm property, an interest in a family farm partnership, or shares in a family farm corporation are bequeathed to a child, grandchild, or great-grandchild of the deceased, there is a complete tax deferral on the transfer, and the child assumes the deceased's tax cost. An election can be made to preclude full or partial deferral of tax, which increases the tax cost of the farm property for the child. Ensure that the $500,000 lifetime capital gains exemption of the deceased has been fully used up, either before or on death, however.

These situations are commonly known as "rollovers." Your heirs assume any potential tax liability for the property, which will be payable only when they dispose of, or are deemed to dispose of, the property.

Optional Tax Returns

If the deceased was the proprietor of, or a partner in, a business, was a beneficiary of a testamentary trust, or had earned "rights or things" (which are generally unrealized income amounts at the date of death), the executor of the estate may have the option of reporting some of the business, trust, or "rights or things" income on three additional, separate returns.

> **Planning Opportunity:** The advantage in filing these separate returns is that each return treats the deceased as a separate person, allowing additional use of tax credits and access to graduated rates of taxation.

Full personal tax credits can be claimed on each return, which can produce a tax saving. The splitting of income among the different returns produces a further saving because of the graduated tax rate system.

Taxation of the Estate

Frequently, income-producing assets are held by the estate in trust before passing to specific beneficiaries. Generally, all income earned and received by the estate from the date of death is taxed in the estate, except for income payable or distributed to beneficiaries, or elected to be attributed to a preferred beneficiary, in which cases it is taxed in the hands of the beneficiaries.

Your will should be drafted to empower the executor of your estate to undertake some testamentary tax planning. For example, controlling the timing of gifts or deciding which assets will pass through the rollover provisions (see below) may reduce taxes in your terminal return and reduce the impact of taxes on your beneficiaries.

Foreign Death Taxes

If you have any assets located in the United States, or if you or any of your beneficiaries is a citizen or resident of the United States, U.S. federal estate tax and state inheritance taxes may apply.

The most recent amendment to the Canada–U.S. Income Tax Convention significantly changed the rules on death taxes with respect to U.S. property. If you own U.S. assets, you should consult with your tax advisor to determine what steps, if any, might be taken to reduce or eliminate the U.S. estate tax exposure.

PLANNING TECHNIQUES

There is often a "cost" involved in implementing some of the estate planning strategies outlined below that goes beyond financial. A tax saving could be accompanied by loss of control over the related asset, or perhaps the overall flexibility of your estate plan will be impaired to some extent. The tools and techniques that you use depend on your personal and financial situation and your estate planning objectives.

Gifting

The most direct method of accomplishing the more common estate planning goals is to gift assets to your potential heirs during your lifetime. Since ownership is transferred, the future capital appreciation of the assets and the related future tax liability are also transferred. There are three drawbacks to gifting, however.

First, if the asset is transferred to your spouse or a related child under the age of 18, you will be subject to the "attribution rules." In other words, any investment income (i.e., interest, dividend, and rental income) earned on the property is taxed in your hands until the marriage breaks down (by death, divorce, or separation) or until the year the child turns 18. Also, when an asset is transferred to your spouse or to a child age 18 or older, the capital gain on the sale of such transferred property is attributed to you.

Second, since ownership of the asset is transferred, you lose control over the asset and you no longer have access to its future income-earning capability.

Third, when you gift an asset to any person, except your spouse, during your lifetime, you generally are deemed to have received proceeds of disposition equal to the fair market value of the asset at that time, and you will be immediately liable for any tax resulting from a capital gain.

As in the case of deemed dispositions that occur on death, there are certain exceptions to the above deemed disposition *inter vivos* (i.e., during your lifetime) rule. You may be able to defer the tax via a rollover when:

- property is transferred to a spouse or a spousal trust (although future capital gains and losses will be attributed back to you), or
- farm property is transferred to a child, grandchild, or great-grandchild.

If you are a shareholder of a Canadian private corporation that uses all or substantially all of the fair market value of its assets in carrying on an active business primarily in Canada, or own qualified farm property, you may be eligible for the $500,000 lifetime capital gains exemption on the disposition of shares of the company (refer to Chapter 8). This exemption may be limited to $400,000 if you have already taken full advantage of the $100,000 cumulative exemption for capital gains realized or deemed to have been realized on other property.

> **Planning Opportunity:** If you have not already used up your $500,000 capital gains exemption, you may want to gift enough of your shares in the private company to your children to trigger a $500,000 capital gain and thereby use the exemption.

This strategy may not make sense if you are planning to sell the company to outsiders, however. It might be better to save the exemption for the arm's length sale, rather than use it for a "paper transaction" between family members. Keep in mind that this exemption could be abolished in the future, as has already occurred with the $100,000 personal capital gains exemption.

Income Splitting

The primary objective of income splitting is to have income that normally would be taxed in your hands, at a high tax rate, taxed instead in the hands of a relative, usually your spouse or child, at a lower tax rate. See Chapter 3 for a definition of income splitting and a discussion of the attribution rules. See also Chapters 12 and 13 for income splitting strategies.

The Use of Trusts

In its simplest form, a trust merely involves the holding of property by one person for the benefit of another person. In more technical terms, a trust is created when a settlor transfers property to a trustee, who holds the property for the benefit of a beneficiary. A trust may be either testamentary (i.e., arising upon your death) or *inter vivos* (i.e., arising during your lifetime).

> **Planning Opportunity:** A trust can allow you to transfer ownership of an asset to an intended heir while you, in the role of trustee of the trust, are able to maintain control over the asset.

Trusts permit you to accomplish a number of your estate planning goals. They may be used for such varied purposes as funding a child's education, providing for handicapped or disabled children, or obtaining professional property management.

Two conditions must be satisfied to achieve a tax saving. First, you must relinquish ownership of the assets held by the trust, although in some cases you may still control the management and operation of the trust itself. Second, you must avoid the attribution rules.

> **Planning Opportunity:** An *inter vivos* trust is generally subject to the same rules as individuals and is taxed at the top personal rate. Testamentary trusts are taxed more favourably at the progressive tax rates applied to individuals.

Because of the difference in the tax treatment of trusts, you must be very selective about the purpose behind creating your trust and the kinds of assets that you place in your trust. For example, if you intend to create a source of future income for your spouse and are considering transferring investment assets to a trust, you might also consider creating a self-directed spousal RRSP. A professional tax advisor can assist you in this choice.

If trust income is distributed to a beneficiary either directly through an actual distribution, or indirectly, as with the preferred beneficiary election (see below), such amounts are deducted from trust income and taxed in the hands of the beneficiary, assuming the attribution rules do not apply. This can result in some tax savings if the beneficiary is taxed at a lower marginal rate.

The *Income Tax Act* provides that certain forms of income earned in a trust retain their character when distributed to beneficiaries and taxed in their hands. For example, eligible Canadian taxable dividends received by a trust and distributed to a beneficiary make the beneficiary eligible for the dividend tax credit.

Preferred Beneficiary Election. When this election is made, income earned by the trust is taxed in the hands of the beneficiary, even though the income remains in the trust. This election is available to beneficiaries entitled to the mental or physical impairment tax credit, or dependent because of such impairment. In addition to the new qualification, a preferred beneficiary must be a Canadian resident and one of the following:

- the settlor of the trust, or his or her spouse or former spouse;
- a child, grandchild, or great-grandchild of the settlor;
- the spouse (but not former spouse) of a child, grandchild, or great-grandchild of the settlor.

The settlor must also contribute more to the trust than any other taxpayer.

The restriction of the preferred beneficiary election to individuals qualifying for the mental or physical impairment credit has curbed the use of trusts for minor children. Some leeway has been granted by Revenue Canada, however. Many trusts empower their trustees to make payments to third parties for the benefit of the beneficiaries. Historically, the concern was that these payments would not qualify as payments to the beneficiaries and the trust would still be responsible for the tax. Revenue Canada will allow third-party payments to qualify as payments to the beneficiaries if the payments are made at the request of the parent/guardian of the child. As a result, a family trust can be structured to pay the discretionary expenses of the beneficiaries while the parent(s) cover the basic necessities of life. Discretionary expenses include tuition for private school, the cost of lessons, memberships, travel, etc.

Revenue Canada will also consider third-party payments paid to cover the necessities of life as payable to the child in very limited circumstances. A trust may pay for the basic necessities of life, either directly to a third party or through reimbursement to the parent/guardian. When calculating its taxable income, the trust may claim a deduction on such payments and the minor beneficiary would include the amount of the payments as income. The parents would not attract any added tax liability, provided that the attribution rules do not apply. Because of the precise nature of these arrangements, you should seek professional advice.

Deemed Disposition Rule for Trusts. Special rules prevent trusts from holding property for an indefinite period. This restriction prevents the long-term deferral of capital gains from income. The general rule provides for a deemed disposition by a trust of all of its capital property every 21 years for proceeds of sale equal to the fair market value of the property. Because the rule is a deeming provision, the proceeds, which might only be on paper, will still affect the trust's tax position.

Estate Freezing

An estate freeze is generally undertaken when an individual owns assets that are likely to increase substantially in value over the long term and wishes to reduce the tax consequences.

An effective freeze can eliminate or defer immediate tax in your hands, ensure that future growth of the asset will benefit your children, and allow you to maintain control of the asset.

An estate freeze is not a gift. If assets are gifted to a child, no value is received in return and control is lost. Under an estate freeze, you retain, or at least have access to, the current value of the frozen assets. Only the future increases in value are transferred to the child. It is also possible for you to retain control over those assets. Unlike estate freezing, gifting assets to your child eliminates tax on your death, but it also may result in an immediate tax liability and probably achieves none of your other estate planning goals.

Direct Sale. Selling an asset to your child, the simplest of estate freezes, may achieve some or even all of your estate planning goals. Tax is eliminated on death, but you must include any capital gain in income for tax purposes in the year of the sale. Normally, you would take back a note payable from the child as payment of the sale price. Through a direct sale, you can dispose of a growth asset and obtain a fixed-value asset in its place. Interest is not required to be charged on the note, although, if this is the case, the attribution rules will apply to any income earned on the transferred asset.

Caution: There are legal issues associated with the sale of an asset to a minor.

With a direct sale, you can claim a reserve (i.e., not recognize the full capital gain) if you have not received all proceeds from the sale and the unpaid proceeds are not yet due. The taxable capital gain must be brought into your income over a specified period, depending on the type of asset sold. When the reserve amount is included in income, it is eligible for the $500,000 lifetime capital gains exemption.

The fact that you are able to demand partial or full payment on the note at any time may represent some form of control over the asset. Transferring the asset to a trust of which the child is a beneficiary may permit you to exercise more control over the asset if you are the trustee.

Corporate Freeze. Because most individuals are concerned with freezing assets that are likely to increase substantially in value in the future, the most common "frozen" assets are business assets. In particular, business assets in the form of shares of a private corporation controlled by the individual are often ideal for a freeze. Using a corporation in an estate freeze provides the individual with considerable flexibility and, if properly structured, enables him or her to achieve each of the estate freezing goals mentioned above.

TAKING ADVANTAGE OF TAX PROVISIONS

Principal Residence Exemption

Detailed rules on the principal residence exemption are contained in Chapter 11. A number of estate planning options involve changes to the ownership of a principal residence.

If two residences are currently owned by a married couple (e.g., a city home and a summer cottage), consider transferring ownership of one property to adult children or grandchildren who reside in the residence for at least part of the year. The more common example is transferring the cottage. This may involve a slight cost currently; for example, tax on the capital gain from the property that has accrued since 1981. Any future gain realized on the disposition of the other property retained by the couple will generally be tax-free under the principal residence rules.

Of course, if you sell or gift the cottage directly to the children, you and your spouse no longer have any legal right to occupy it. Taking back a demand note as consideration on the sale may give you some control over the property, but perhaps not enough to suit your wishes. One solution might be to give the property to a discretionary trust for you and your children. The trust agreement could be structured to permit you to give the cottage to a particular child at some time in the future, while ensuring that the future increase in value accrues to the ultimate owner.

Registered Retirement Savings Plans

RRSPs are probably the most common tax deferral vehicles in use today (also refer to Chapter 14). The immediate tax benefit of an RRSP is that it reduces annual income for tax purposes (within specified limits) by the amount of the annual contribution. The longer-term benefit is that it shelters the income accumulating in the plan from taxation. For estate planning purposes, an RRSP provides you with a fund that, on your death, might be passed to your spouse, who may be subject to a lower tax rate, and, in certain circumstances, to your children.

Spouse and Spousal Trust Rollovers

If you bequeath capital property directly to your spouse or a qualifying spousal trust, the property can be rolled over (i.e., transferred) at your tax cost with no resulting taxation at the time of your death. For these spousal rollover rules to apply, certain criteria must be met:

- You must have been resident in Canada immediately before death.
- The ownership of the property must actually be transferred to your spouse or a qualifying spousal trust.
- If the transfer is to your spouse, he or she must have been resident in Canada immediately prior to your death.
- The spousal trust must be testamentary (i.e., created by your will) and must be resident in Canada when the property vests in the trust.

- Vesting in the spouse or spousal trust generally must occur within 36 months of your death.
- If the property is transferred to a spousal trust, your spouse must be entitled to receive all the income during his or her lifetime and no other person may receive or have the use of any income or capital during that period.

A certain amount of planning can be undertaken after death by your estate's executor. For example, he or she may elect that the spousal rollover provisions not apply to selected assets. This election will enable your executor to use previous years' losses and, if the election is made in respect of qualified property, your $500,000 capital gains exemption, both of which will reduce the future tax liability of your spouse.

Life Insurance

Life insurance plays an important role in estate planning. It can be used for a variety of purposes:

- to provide a base for generating investment income to replace earnings;
- as a tax-sheltered investment vehicle, if properly structured, for the accumulation of funds during your lifetime, with a tax-free payout on your death to your beneficiaries;
- to help the surviving shareholder of a closely held corporation finance the purchase of shares from the estate or heirs of a deceased shareholder;
- to provide liquidity on death to cover the payment of income taxes and other debts and expenses;
- to provide additional assets to bequeath to children who are not involved in a family business. In the absence of the insurance funds, those children might otherwise receive shares of the family business, creating a possible disruption in the operation of the business.

> ☑ **Planning Opportunity:** Insurance proceeds payable as a result of the death of the insured are not subject to income tax in the hands of the beneficiary.

Your financial situation and the future needs of your family will dictate the type and quantity of life insurance you should have. While your insurance agent can provide you with details of the wide variety of individual policies available, bear in mind that there are two basic types of life insurance: term policies and permanent policies.

The term policy is generally less expensive for a younger person, but has a number of disadvantages. For example, you receive no benefits if the policy is cancelled either by the insurer or yourself. There is usually no obligation for an insurer to continue coverage, and the policy likely will not be renewed beyond a certain age. Of course, insurance companies now offer many variations on the term policy that have additional features, such as options that guarantee your insurability to almost any age.

While a permanent policy (often referred to as a "whole life" or "universal" policy) initially involves higher premiums, it has the advantage of also serving as an investment vehicle. For example, you may usually borrow against your insurance savings at a favourable rate, and you may receive a lump sum if you decide to cash in the policy at a future date. Most permanent policies are structured so that accruing income is not taxed annually; however, borrowing against the cash surrender value or "cashing in" the policy could result in tax.

Insurance arrangements involving the purchase of a deceased shareholder's shares by the surviving shareholders are more complex and require careful planning.

SUCCESSION AND ESTATE PLANNING FOR BUSINESS ASSETS

If you are a business owner or have an interest in a business, this asset could be your largest source of current as well as retirement income. Converting your business interest into retirement income requires the implementation of a succession plan. You may foresee eventually transferring control of the business to your children, or you may wish to sell the business to a partner or third party on your retirement, or arrange for professional management while ownership remains with your family. Whatever your goals, you should be aware of the planning techniques that can result in substantial tax savings for you and your family.

Most financial planning, including tax and succession planning, involves incorporated businesses. If your business is not incorporated, but can be, you should discuss the situation with your professional advisor to determine if you would benefit from such a change in business structure.

Before choosing the planning techniques best suited to you, there are a number of considerations you should examine. You should consider the abilities of your spouse and/or children to manage the business, their relative participation in control and ownership, the time frame for transfer of control, the role of key employees, and your own financial needs after retirement.

 Planning Opportunity: The remainder of this chapter examines three major succession and estate planning techniques that focus on business assets:

- exemption of the tax on capital gains on the transfer of shares of an eligible small business corporation and deferral and/or exemption of tax on capital gains on the transfer of eligible farm property to your children;
- methods of corporate estate freezing so that the tax consequences of all or part of future growth in the business are passed to your heirs;
- the use of insurance to fund certain succession planning transactions.

Exemption of Tax on Capital Gains on Shares of Small Business Corporations

The deemed disposition rules consider shares to be disposed of for proceeds equal to fair market value immediately before death. As well, on the gifting of the shares to anyone other than your spouse, you are deemed to receive proceeds of disposition equal to the fair market value of the shares.

If the value of the business has increased significantly over the years, a large capital gain will generally result from the transfer of the corporation's shares. Such a gain is eligible for the lifetime $500,000 capital gains exemption. If you owned capital property prior to 1994, you may already have claimed the $100,000 personal capital gains exemption. In this case, your lifetime exemption is restricted to $400,000. This exemption applies to gains realized on the disposition of "qualified farm property" or "qualified small business corporation shares," terms defined in the *Income Tax Act*. Generally speaking, if your business is an active business carried on primarily in Canada, and at least 90 per cent of the fair market value of assets of the corporation are used in the business, chances are that it would qualify for the $500,000 capital gains exemption. If your spouse owns part of the small business corporation, he or she also has a $500,000 exemption, which means that tax on up to $1 million of capital gains may be eliminated. If the gain is realized in one year, however, you may be subject to the Alternative Minimum Tax (AMT) on the "untaxed" part of the gain.

The Alternative Minimum Tax. The AMT is an alternative method for calculating income tax. It was created in 1986 to prevent high-income Canadians from sheltering taxable income with deductions, credits, and shelters. The AMT should always be considered in tax planning, particularly if the taxpayer has claimed a rollover or where a significant capital gain has occurred. You must calculate your taxable income using both the regular and AMT methods for the current year and pay the greater tax amount. Under the AMT, the untaxed portion of any capital gain is added back. Some relief is available if you are able to claim that the income or deduction that gave rise to AMT was a result of timing. Any overpaid AMT can be carried forward seven years against your future tax liability to the extent that regular income tax exceeds AMT. In addition, AMT does not apply in the year of death.

NEW **New for 1998!** The AMT no longer applies to registered pension plan (RPP) and registered retirement savings plan (RRSP) contributions. This change is retroactive to 1994. Taxpayers who are planning to make catch-up contributions to their RRSPs will benefit.

Rollover of Farming Property

To encourage the children of farmers to continue to operate the family farm after their parents' retirement or death, special rules permit the transfer of farming assets from one generation to the next without incurring a tax cost. Similar rollover rules also apply to the transfer of shares of a family farm corporation (or a holding corporation that owns such shares) and to the transfer of an interest in a family farm partnership. Also, the $500,000 capital gains exemption is available for gains realized on the disposition of qualified farm property, to the extent that it has not been used to shelter gains from the disposition of qualified small business corporation shares.

Rollover provisions do not eliminate taxation, but merely postpone the taxation of a gain. However, transferring the property under the lifetime exemption will increase the child's tax cost of the property, resulting in a smaller capital gain when the child does dispose of the property. The child may use the $500,000 lifetime exemption when the property is sold, provided the exemption still exists at that time.

Estate Freezing Techniques for Corporate Assets

After deciding on the objectives that best suit your estate planning needs, particular techniques must be chosen that will achieve your intended objectives with the optimum tax advantage. The techniques briefly discussed below all involve "freezing" the present value of your business so that all or part of the future growth and the resulting tax consequences are deferred to your heirs. These techniques may also be used, however, to freeze the value of almost any assets having inherent taxable capital gains.

Recall that an estate freeze is a method of organizing your affairs to permit any future appreciation in the value of selected assets to accrue to others, usually your children, and not to you. From your tax perspective, the value of the asset is frozen on the day of the transaction. Because these freezing techniques involve corporate assets, seek professional advice before undertaking any of these strategies.

The choice of technique used to freeze the assets will depend on a number of considerations, including:

- nature of the assets to be frozen;
- size of the estate;
- extent of control you wish to exercise over the frozen assets;
- number of parties to be involved in the freeze;
- immediate tax cost, if any, that might result from the freeze, taking into account the $500,000 lifetime capital gains exemption on qualified property;
- your tolerance for complexity in your financial arrangements;
- professional fees that will be incurred;
- degree of flexibility and reversibility desired.

The following discussion assumes that your active business assets are owned by a corporation controlled by you. In general, the corporate structure facilitates effective succession and estate planning. If business assets are not held by such a corporation, it is usually a relatively simple matter to arrange under professional guidance.

Direct Sale. Perhaps the simplest method of freezing your interest in shares of a privately held company is to sell the shares directly to your adult children. The sale would take place at fair market value, and you would take back a promissory note for the balance of the sale price not received in cash. There should be an agreement of purchase and sale that sets out the details of the sale, such as terms of payment, the due date of any unpaid amount, whether the unpaid balance is subject to interest, etc. Although it is not necessary to charge interest on the unpaid balance owed by your children, you should be aware that the attribution rules will apply if no interest is charged.

There are some disadvantages to a direct sale. You will be taxed on any capital gain realized in excess of any gain eligible for your $500,000 lifetime capital gains exemption. You also may become subject to the Alternative Minimum Tax. However, you may claim a reserve (i.e., exclude from income) on a portion of the taxable gain if you do not immediately receive all proceeds of disposition. When amounts claimed under the reserve provisions are eventually brought back into income for tax purposes, they will be eligible for your $500,000 lifetime capital gains exemption. Remember that even if you gift the shares to your children, you will be deemed to have received proceeds of disposition equal to the fair market value of those shares.

A second disadvantage of a direct sale is that you could lose control of the business if sufficient voting shares are sold to your children. This may be overcome if you subscribe for new voting preferred shares that carry more votes than the existing common shares. Alternatively, you may be able to exercise some control by placing the common shares in escrow (i.e., maintaining possession and control of them) until the demand note has been entirely paid off.

Another disadvantage of a direct sale is that unless cash is paid for the shares, the amount owing to you remains in the corporation and may therefore continue to be at risk. To get around this, have your children take out a loan to pay for the shares, rather than accepting a demand note from them. Accepting the full payment would necessitate recognizing the entire capital gain almost immediately for tax purposes, however, and risks triggering the

Alternative Minimum Tax. As a compromise, the consideration could be part cash (from the outside loan) and part note (from the children).

Sale to a Holding Company. A common method of freezing the value of shares in an existing company involves the use of a new holding company specifically set up to acquire such shares. The children involved in the freeze would incorporate a company and acquire all its common shares for a nominal amount. You would transfer your shares in the operating company to the newly incorporated holding company, which generally can be done on a tax-deferred basis. You would take back voting preferred shares (with a value equal to the shares transferred into the holding company) in the new company as consideration for the transfer.

> ⚠ **Caution:** Over the last few years, changes have been made to family law in certain provinces requiring the equal division upon marital breakdown of assets acquired by a couple during their marriage. This requirement could result in a significant portion of a parent's assets being transferred to the former spouse of a child.

To avoid this possibility, the parent could acquire all the common shares of the holding company as well as the preferred shares. The parent would then gift the common shares to his or her children. Making a gift would exclude the common shares from the matrimonial property of the married child in most instances, because assets inherited or received by way of gift are excluded from matrimonial property. In Quebec, shares of a private or public company are not included in matrimonial property. In certain provinces, an appropriately worded deed of gift can also exclude from matrimonial property any income derived from the gifted property (such as dividends on gifted shares).

Any future appreciation in the value of the business operations now accrues to your children. You could retain control of the operating company by holding voting preferred shares in the holding company. This permits you to set dividends and a reasonable salary according to your income requirements and allows you to run the business much as you did before.

One disadvantage of the use of a holding company in an estate freeze is that a capital gain or deemed dividend may arise on the redemption or disposition of the preferred shares (that you acquired as consideration for the transfer of your shares) during your lifetime. All or a portion of the capital gain could be exempt under your $500,000 lifetime capital gains exemption, however, if the shares were considered qualified property at the time of redemption or disposal. It might be necessary to obtain a professional valuation of your shares.

Asset Freeze. As an alternative to transferring the shares of an operating company to a holding company, you may wish to consider freezing the value of these shares by selling the underlying operating assets to a new company incorporated by your children. This method of estate freezing may involve considerable work and expense, and sales or other transfer taxes could result. However, in some situations an asset freeze is the best approach. It works well if you own a multifaceted business and you want to break it up into separate corporations, each to be owned by one child.

Internal Freeze. It may be possible to reorganize the existing share capital structure of your company to accomplish an estate freeze. Where applicable provincial or federal company law permits, you may exchange all your existing common shares for voting preferred shares of a certain type. After the exchange, a new class of common shares would be created and purchased by the children at a nominal amount. The result of such a reorganization is that you freeze the current value of your holdings in the operating company, and your children participate in the future growth in value of the company through their ownership of the common shares. This type of freeze is relatively simple, does not require a new corporate entity, and provides you with preferred shares that should give you a fixed income, if desired. Of course, as with other freezes where no cash is received, there is always the problem that the money owed to you is tied up in the corporation and therefore exposed to some risk.

Choosing the Best Freeze Vehicle. The freeze vehicle you will ultimately choose should not be based solely on income tax considerations. For example, a partial estate freeze should provide better protection from future inflation than a complete freeze. In all cases, consult your professional advisor before making a final decision. An estate freeze requires careful planning, not only because of the tax consequences involved, but also because it may be difficult to thaw (i.e., unwind).

Sales to Third Parties. If you own a business, you may want to transfer it to unrelated parties, such as fellow shareholders, partners, or key employees, rather than to your children or spouse. Your spouse or children may not be able or willing to run the business, or the partners or other shareholders may not want the children involved.

Selling your shares to your fellow shareholders will ensure that the company remains private and thus eligible for the small business tax benefits.

Arranging a sale to employees may bind your best employees to the business, relieve you of some management headaches as you get older, and assist in an orderly transfer of ownership. A sale could be coupled with a long-term employment contract should you wish to remain involved in the company.

Insurance

Insurance arrangements for business purposes are complex and require careful planning. The purpose of business insurance in the context of estate planning is to ensure that there are sufficient funds on hand at your death for the business to be dealt with in accordance with your wishes.

Depending on your estate plan, a properly constructed insurance plan will ensure that your estate has sufficient liquid assets on hand to pay tax on any taxable capital gains realized on your death. Furthermore, such a plan will enable your partner or another shareholder in the corporation to purchase your share of the business on your death, if that is your wish.

Buy-Sell Agreements. A buy-sell agreement is basically a contract between business partners or shareholders of a corporation. It is frequently used in estate planning to extend to surviving shareholders the right or obligation to purchase the shares of a deceased shareholder. It is advantageous both for the surviving shareholders, who may not want a stranger to buy into the corporation, and for the family of the deceased, who might otherwise have difficulty selling the shares.

The spousal rollover rules are not applicable to shares that are subject to a compulsory buy-sell agreement. Tax is paid by the deceased shareholder in the terminal tax return on any resulting capital gain if the $500,000 lifetime capital gains exemption cannot be fully used. If the buy-sell agreement is structured in such a way that the surviving shareholder has an option to buy, and the surviving spouse has an option to sell, the shares can first pass to the spouse on a rollover basis. Any capital gain arising on the subsequent sale of the shares by the spouse would be recognized in his or her hands. The gains would, however, be eligible for the spouse's own $500,000 lifetime capital gains exemption, if still available and provided that the shares are qualified shares at the time.

Whichever buy-sell method is employed, one thing remains certain—unless there is some method of funding the transaction, the agreement may not be consummated. It is common for life insurance to be used to provide the funds to finance the sale, and there are three common methods of employing life insurance as the funding mechanism for a buy-sell agreement.

- *Criss-Cross Insurance.* This is an insurance arrangement where each shareholder of a corporation acquires a life insurance policy on the life of each other shareholder. On the death of one shareholder, the survivors receive the tax-free proceeds of the policy and use the funds to purchase the deceased's shares from his or her estate or beneficiaries. One disadvantage of this method is that the cost of the insurance to each shareholder can vary widely depending on the ages and health of the other shareholders.

- *Corporate-Owned Insurance.* With this type of policy, the corporation insures the lives of its shareholders and receives the proceeds on their deaths. The advantage of this method is that the corporation pays all insurance premiums and the cost to the shareholders is shared in proportion to their shareholdings. The proceeds are used by the corporation to purchase the deceased's shares, either from the deceased's estate or from the surviving spouse. Generally, neither the deceased nor the spouse will be subject to tax on the buyback if the arrangement is properly structured. Specifically, the surviving shareholders will avoid an increase in the cost base of their shares upon redemption, which in effect means the deceased shareholder's gain has been transferred to them. This situation could be compensated for by reducing the redemption price so that more cash is retained in the corporation or by increasing the amount of the insurance coverage.

  Pending changes to legislation could make this kind of arrangement less attractive because the deceased would be subject to tax. The changes are complex, however, and transitional rules offer protection in certain circumstances. Existing succession plans should be reviewed to see if they qualify for the protection, while business reorganizations should be structured to alleviate the impact of the new rules. Obtaining professional advice is strongly recommended.

- *Split-Dollar Insurance.* Split-dollar insurance is a combination of both criss-cross and corporate-owned insurance. Each shareholder purchases a whole-life type of policy on the other and assigns the cash value of the policy to the company. On the death of a shareholder, the company receives the cash value of the policy while the surviving shareholders receive the face value less the cash value, and use these proceeds to purchase the shares. The advantage of this method is that the company pays most of the premiums.

The use of buy-sell agreements, combined with life insurance funding, should be considered where shares of private companies are owned and there are two or more shareholders dealing with each other at arm's length and also in some non-arm's length situations. In all cases, the insuring method employed should not be chosen without the assistance of a professional advisor.

BEGINNING THE PROCESS

Estate planning is not a once-and-for-all exercise. You should view it as an ongoing process, involving a variety of techniques over the years, designed to suit your changing circumstances. This chapter has focused on the tax aspects of estate planning. There are other factors to consider that are of equal or greater importance. Above all, don't rush into a tax-motivated estate plan without giving full consideration to your personal and financial circumstances. Keep in mind that few things in life turn out exactly as we plan them. Your estate plan must have sufficient flexibility built into it so that you can adapt it to fit unforeseen future events.

Tax Planning—You and the GST/HST/QST

All Canadians must pay a 7 per cent Goods and Services Tax (GST) (or a 15 per cent Harmonized Sales Tax [HST] in Nova Scotia, New Brunswick, and Newfoundland and Labrador) on most goods and services. In Quebec there is also a 7.5 per cent Quebec Sales Tax (QST).

THE BASICS

To receive a rebate of any GST/HST and QST paid, you must be a registrant. Although not all taxpayers can take advantage of the rebates, certain individuals (e.g., employees and members of a partnership) may, under specific conditions, qualify for a rebate of the GST/HST and QST paid, even if they are not registrants. These individuals may obtain this rebate by filing a special form with their income tax return. The rebate is available only for those expenses that are deductible when calculating income for income tax purposes. A rebate factor of 7/107

(15/115 in the HST provinces) is used to calculate the qualifying portion of net expenses (7.5/107.5 for the QST rebate).

Taxpayers must remember to include the GST/HST (or QST) rebate in the computation of their income for the taxation year in which the rebate is received. For example, a rebate claimed in the 1997 income tax return, but received in 1998, must be included in the taxpayer's 1998 income.

WHO MAY CLAIM A REBATE?

Only the employees of a registrant employer and the members of a registered partnership may claim the rebate, provided the registrants are not otherwise entitled to a rebate of the GST/HST and QST on the same eligible expense. For example, an employee of a non-profit organization is entitled to claim the rebate only if the organization is a registrant.

Commissioned and other salespeople, and employees and partners who have expenses related to a motor vehicle are the most common claimants for GST/HST and QST rebates.

 Caution: An employee cannot claim the GST rebate if his or her employer is a listed financial institution.

This restriction means that a salesperson who works on commission at a brokerage firm or an insurance company is not eligible for the GST/HST rebate on the expenses that he or she deducts when calculating income. This restriction does not apply to the QST rebate.

WHAT EXPENSES ARE ELIGIBLE?

The rebate is available solely for expenses deducted for income tax purposes in the computation of a taxpayer's employment income, or income from a partnership.

Some expenses that would normally be eligible for a rebate are entertainment expenses (50% of the amount), advertising costs, professional membership dues, office expenses, leasing costs, various supplies, automobile expenses, and capital cost allowance (CCA) on a motor vehicle, a musical instrument, or an aircraft. If the rebate is in respect of the capital cost of property, the rebate reduces the capital cost of the property at the time the rebate is received (usually the following year), rather than being included in income.

Expenses for which a reasonable allowance was paid by an employer are not eligible for a tax rebate. An employee or partner can, however, claim a GST/HST (or a QST) rebate if the allowance received was unreasonable (i.e., one that must be included in the employee's or partner's income). In such cases, the employee or partner must obtain a statement from the employer or partnership to that effect.

FILING AN APPLICATION

In general, a rebate application (form GST-370 for the GST/HST, and form VD-358 for the QST) is filed with the income tax return for the calendar year in which the expenses are incurred, although a claim can be made retroactively within four years after that calendar year.

In general, when computing the rebate, the consideration for an expense corresponds to the amount paid, which includes the amount of GST/HST (or QST) paid. Partners can claim a GST/HST or QST rebate using a calendar year, rather than the year-end of the partnership, if they deduct the expenses for income tax purposes on a calendar-year basis.

The following example illustrates how the GST and QST rebates are calculated.

Computing the Rebate			
	Salesperson's Expenses	GST Rebate Computed on	QST Rebate Computed on
Entertainment	$ 800	$ 400	$ 400
Office expenses:			
Electricity	400	400	400
Property taxes	200	—	—
Insurance	300	—	—
Suppliers	100	100	100
Automobile expenses:			
CCA	1,000	1,000	1,000[1]
Interest	200	—	—
Insurance	400	—	—
Operating costs	150	150	150
Repairs and maintenance	150	150	150
	$3,700	$2,200	$2,200

[1] The CCA on the car is eligible for the QST rebate if the car was purchased after July 31, 1995. No QST rebate is available unless this condition is met. Since the car in this example was purchased after July 31, 1995, the CCA qualifies for a QST rebate.

Notes

- The vendor is entitled to a GST rebate of $144 (7/107 of $2,200) and a QST rebate of $145 (7.5/107.5 of $1,200 and 6.5/106.5 of $1,000).
- Since property taxes, insurance and interest are not subject to GST, no rebate is allowed. In Quebec, there is a tax on insurance premiums, but there is no entitlement to a rebate.
- The portion of the GST and QST rebates that relates to the expenses ($79 and $84, respectively) must be included in the income of the employee for income tax purposes, whereas another portion (CCA on automobile) equal to $65 and $61, respectively, reduces the capital cost on which the CCA is based.

Filing Time

TAX CREDITS VERSUS DEDUCTIONS

The difference between a tax credit and a tax deduction can be described simply. A tax deduction decreases taxable income, and saves tax based on the marginal tax bracket. A tax credit is an amount subtracted to arrive at the actual tax due. It is not part of the calculation of taxable income.

A combined federal and provincial tax credit of $100 will result in a tax saving of $100, regardless of the individual's marginal tax bracket. A $100 expenditure that results in a tax deduction will save an individual in a 45 per cent bracket $45, but will save an individual in a 26 per cent bracket only $26.

Tax credits provide the same dollar benefit to each taxpayer claiming a particular credit because the credit is subtracted directly from the individual's tax payable. If, however, the individual has no tax payable from which the credit can be deducted, and the credit is not refundable, the value of the credit is lost.

While many of us have some degree of familiarity with the personal credits listed in our tax returns, the rules for many of the credits are modified and updated regularly. In this chapter, we list the various personal tax credits available to all Canadians. With the exception of the single status and medical expenses tax credits, most of the credits and deductions are discussed in detail in other chapters that deal with specific tax topics.

PERSONAL TAX CREDITS FOR CANADIANS

The credits discussed below represent only the federal portion of the tax credits. Most provinces, with the exception of Quebec, calculate provincial income taxes based on federal income tax payable. Therefore, each taxpayer, except residents of Quebec, will receive an additional benefit through a reduction in provincial income taxes payable. For example, in Ontario the combined tax reduction of the single status tax credit for a taxpayer in the top tax bracket is approximately $1,903.

For All Taxpayers
Single Status. The federal single status tax credit for all individuals for 1998 is $1,098. The federal credit is indexed annually according to increases in the Consumer Price Index above 3 per cent.

NEW **New for 1998!** The 1998 federal budget introduced an additional credit of $85 for low- and middle-income Canadians, effective July 1, 1998. The maximum federal single status tax credit for qualifying individuals will be $1,183. For a single person, the credit will be reduced where income is over $6,956 and fully eliminated when income is more than $19,456. In addition, the federal surtax of 3 per cent is being eliminated for all taxpayers with incomes below about $50,000 per year. For individuals with incomes between about $50,000 and $65,000, the surtax will be reduced. For 1998, individuals will receive half of the full value of the 1999 surtax reduction.

Medical Expenses. The federal medical expenses tax credit for 1998 is calculated by subtracting the lesser of $1,614 or 3 per cent of your net income for the year from your total qualifying medical expenses. The result is then multiplied by 17 per cent to arrive at the final credit value. (The $1,614 amount is indexed annually according to increases in the Consumer Price Index above 3 per cent.) Receipts for the medical expenses must be filed when claiming the tax credit, and the expenses must not have been claimed in a previous return. If the claimant dies within the year, the medical expenses must be paid within any 24-month period, including the date of death. In any other case, they must be paid within any 12-month period ending in the taxation year.

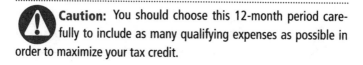 **Caution:** You should choose this 12-month period carefully to include as many qualifying expenses as possible in order to maximize your tax credit.

The *Income Tax Act* contains extensive provisions detailing the nature of expenditures that qualify as medical expenses, which include the following services and products:

- medicine;
- dentistry;
- osteopathy;
- chiropody or podiatry;
- chiropractic;
- naturopathy, including acupuncturists;
- dietetics;
- therapeutic science (physiotherapy and occupational therapy);
- optometry;
- psychoanalysis;
- psychology;
- Christian Science;
- pathological or audiological speech therapy;
- a maximum of $1,000 or 50 per cent of the value of an air conditioner, humidifier, or air cleaner necessary to help an individual cope with chronic ailments, disease, or disorder;
- 20 per cent (to a $5,000 maximum) of the costs of adapting a van to transport a wheelchair-bound individual;
- sign language interpreter fees;
- expenses incurred to alter the driveway of an individual's principal residence, where the individual has a severe and prolonged mobility impairment, to allow the individual access to a bus;
- expenses incurred for moving to accessible housing (to a $2,000 maximum);
- part-time attendant care up to $10,000 per year ($20,000 in the year of death).

NEW **New for 1998!** The 1998 federal budget proposed to allow as an eligible medical expense reasonable expenses related to the training of an individual in connection with providing care to an individual with a mental or physical infirmity. To be eligible for the credit, the taxpayer must be providing care to an individual who is related to the taxpayer and that individual must have a mental or physical infirmity and be a member of the taxpayer's household or dependent on the taxpayer for support.

Specifically excluded from this credit are the following products and services:

- toothpaste;
- non-prescription birth control devices;
- wigs, unless they have been made for an individual who has suffered extreme hair loss as a result of disease, treatment, or accident;
- maternity clothing;
- antiseptic diaper services;
- funeral expenses;
- illegal medical treatments or operations;
- food and beverages, unless they must be ingested as treatment for an illness;
- gym, spa, or hotel health programs;
- scales for weighing food;
- payments to a municipality, in cases where the municipality has employed a doctor to administer to the community.

Refundable Medical Tax Credit. In addition to the normal non-refundable medical expense tax credit, eligible individuals are also entitled to claim a refundable tax credit for the year equal to the lesser of $500 or 25 per cent of eligible medical expenses. The credit is reduced by 5 per cent of adjusted income exceeding $16,069. Individuals eligible for the credit must be Canadian residents and have income of at least $2,500 for the year.

For Employees (See Chapter 7)
CPP/QPP and Employment Insurance contributions

For Taxpayers with Spouses (See Chapter 12)
Spouse credit
Mental or physical impairment
Tuition fees

Education
Infirm dependant
Age 65 and over
Pension income

For Taxpayers with Children (See Chapter 13)

Infirm dependant
Mental or physical impairment
Tuition fees
Education
Equivalent-to-spouse

For Seniors (See Chapter 16)

Age 65 and over
Pension income
Mental or physical impairment

For Canadians with Elderly Parents (See Chapter 17)

Equivalent-to-spouse
Infirm dependant
Mental or physical impairment
Caregiver

For Canadians Who Make Charitable or Political Contributions (See Chapter 18)

Charitable donations
Political contributions

TAX FILING TIME—THE ESSENTIAL ELEMENTS

Will EFILING and TELEFILING Save You Time?

Electronic filing (EFILING) is a relatively new innovation from Revenue Canada that allows individual Canadians to submit their annual tax returns electronically. The software required is not yet available for the home, which means that you must EFILE through a third-party EFILE service provider. In 1997, Revenue Canada estimated that there were 11,000 EFILE service providers. A recognized EFILE service provider must display the EFILE symbol.

Revenue Canada boasts a two-week turnaround time for EFILED returns. Although you are not required to submit receipts and forms with your EFILED return, you are still required to keep them, as well as a copy of your return, on file. Revenue Canada will inform your service provider which forms or receipts you are required to submit.

The EFILING system provides a quick and paper-free method for creating and processing the annual tax return for individuals who already consult a third party. During peak tax preparation times, in particular during the month of April, the quicker turnaround time definitely is a benefit.

TELEFILING is a service that individual taxpayers can take advantage of from home. You must use the TELEFILE Access Code, which is the four-digit number printed below your social insurance number on the pre-printed address label sent to your home. Revenue Canada intended this service to be used only by individuals who have very simple returns (i.e., those who earn only pension or employment income). You enter your personal tax information at the prompts provided on the TELEFILE telephone system. If you had a complicated return, the service would take up far too much telephone time during the peak filing periods. The service is only available from January 1 to April 30 of the year you file your return. Again, you must retain all of your receipts in the event that Revenue Canada asks you to verify your return information.

This system is only truly useful for individuals who have a very simple return. In fact, unless you are assigned a TELEFILE Access Code, you cannot access the system at all. The determination of whether you receive a code is based on your previous year's return. Finally, because the system is only offered during the peak tax filing period, you may encounter delays due to busy telephone lines.

Amending Your Previous Years' Returns

You are required by law to keep your tax records and documentation for the six previous years. At first glance, this might seem like a needless hassle, but there is also an opportunity here. If you find, as a result of implementing a tax plan, that you did not take advantage of certain deductions or credits, or you made a mistake in a previous year's return, you can resubmit your revised return. There is a time limit, however. In most instances, Revenue Canada will reassess for errors or omissions within three years of the original filing date, even if the reassessment would be in the taxpayer's favour. Beyond this limit, Revenue Canada has discretion under the Fairness Package to reassess a taxation year at the request of a taxpayer.

A Word on Tax Audits

Similarly, the tax authorities have three years from the time your tax return is initially assessed to review the information and make any reassessment of your taxes. Although there is an excellent chance that you never will be audited, it is important to be able to explain the information on your return if you are asked. For this reason, good record-keeping is an essential element of your tax planning. You need to document the intent and the details of your various transactions and all aspects of your business and financial activities. This documentation will assist you in remembering in several years' time exactly what occurred. Should you be audited, this detailed documentation will provide evidence of careful and businesslike planning, an important protective stance in an audit.

There is no need to fear a tax audit if your tax plans are well-designed and well-documented in accordance with tax law. If you have made misrepresentations through neglect, carelessness, or wilful default, or if you have committed fraud, however, you do have something to worry about. There is no time limit for assessment on such activities.

If You Are an Employee

For Canadians who earn income solely from employment sources, the best tax planning advice is that you must ensure that you use all credits, deductions, and tax deferral options available to you. For the most part, if you are a Canadian employee, you have limited opportunities for tax planning because you don't control the timing of your income.

EMPLOYMENT INCOME—WHAT IS INCLUDED?

Your taxable employment income in most cases will include any benefit you receive by virtue of that employment. These amounts are measured by your employer and reported to you and to the government on your T4 (Relevé 1 in Quebec) each year.

Fringe Benefits

Included in your taxable employment income are such things as personal use of an employer's auto, certain premiums paid by your employer under provincial hospitalization and medical-care plans, prizes and incentive awards, financial counselling, travel benefits, and the total cost of group life insurance. Non-taxable benefits include such things as subsidized meals, uniforms or special clothing required for the job, recreational facilities provided at your work location, discounts on merchandise you purchase from your employer for personal use, retirement or re-employment counselling, mental or physical health counselling, and private health and income insurance plans.

Although there is less planning flexibility with employment income as compared to other sources of income, there are various compensation alternatives that may be available to you through your employer. The following outlines these alternatives and their tax implications.

Employee Loans

The term "employee loan" is something of a misnomer, since it is broadly defined. It describes any situation in which the employee is indebted in some way to the employer. The employee is taxed on any imputed interest benefit resulting from this indebtedness. The benefit rules apply not only to loans, but also to any other form of debt incurred by virtue of the previous, current, or future office or employment of an individual. It is not necessary that the employee be the debtor, nor is there any requirement that the employer be the creditor. For example, the imputed interest rules will apply if the employer makes a loan to the employee's child to help support his or her university education, or if an employee obtains a bank loan at a below-market interest rate due to the employer's involvement.

Regardless of the actual debtor, any imputed interest benefit will be taxable in the hands of the employee. The rules also apply to third-party loans where the employer is financing part or all of the cost of the loan.

Caution: The amount of the taxable benefit included in income is generally calculated as the difference between interest that would be paid using the prevailing prescribed interest rate, set by the government each quarter, and interest actually paid within the year or 30 days after the end of the calendar year.

If you borrow $10,000 from your employer at 2 per cent and the prescribed rate is 5 per cent all year, you must include $300 in income as a taxable benefit (5 per cent minus 2 per cent times $10,000), assuming the loan is outstanding for the entire year.

Commercial Rate Rule Exception. The taxable benefit rules do not apply to an employee loan on which interest is charged at a rate equal to or above the commercial lending rate at the time the loan was made. This exception may be restricted depending on all the terms and conditions of the loan.

Home Purchase Loans. A qualifying home purchase loan can be made to an employee or a related person for the purpose of acquiring a dwelling or to refinance a mortgage on such a dwelling. The borrower or the related person must live in the dwelling. The definition of a "home purchase loan" includes a loan used to acquire a share of a cooperative housing corporation entitling the purchaser or a related person to inhabit a dwelling unit in the cooperative.

The taxable benefit on home purchase loans arises if the interest charged on the loan by the employer is less than the prescribed amount for the date the loan was made. The prescribed rate for this purpose for 1998 was 4 per cent for the first quarter of the year and 5 per cent for the last three quarters of the year. All home purchase loans are considered to have a term not exceeding five years. On each fifth anniversary date of the loan, a new loan is deemed to be received, and the prescribed rate of interest at that time is compared to the prescribed rates for the next five-year period.

Planning Opportunity: Because of the way the prescribed rate is calculated, we know in advance what the rate will be in the following quarter. An employee who is arranging a loan from an employer to acquire (or to repay a loan that was used to acquire) a home should request a short-term loan initially (i.e., less than three months). If the prescribed rate for the next quarter is lower than (or the same as) the current quarter, another short-term loan can be arranged. If the prescribed rate is showing a tendency to rise over an extended period, a long-term (e.g., five-year) loan could be finalized in the current quarter.

Home Relocation Loans. Since mid-1985, a deduction has been available to employees who relocate or take up a new position, provided they are eligible to claim moving expenses (discussed below) and have received a low-interest or interest-free loan to assist with the acquisition of a home at the new location. The deduction is made from any taxable benefit relating to this home purchase loan when taxable income is calculated. The deduction is equal to the lesser of the actual benefit included in income and the benefit from a $25,000 interest-free employee loan. There is a time limit: this deduction will be available for the lesser of five years or the length of time the home purchase loan (or a replacement loan for it) is outstanding.

As a result of a 1966 Federal Court of Appeal case (*Siwik* v. *The Queen*, 96 DTC 1678), it may be possible to argue that a low-interest or non-interest-bearing loan or advance by an employer made prior to February 24, 1998 is not subject to the imputed interest rules because the loan/advance was not made because of, or as a consequence of, the employment, but as a consequence of the move.

NEW **New for 1998!** The 1998 federal budget eliminated the tax-exempt status of employers' mortgage-interest subsidy payments paid to relocated employees. Additionally, benefits paid by employers to relocating employees to reimburse them for losses incurred on the sale of the former residence are no longer tax-exempt unless they total less than $15,000. Half of any amount in excess of $15,000 will be included in the taxable income of the employee. If you started work at your new location on or before September 30, 1998, these provisions will not apply to you until 2001.

CREDITS AND DEDUCTIONS

CPP/QPP and Employment Insurance Credit

The federal CPP/QPP and EI tax credit is calculated as 17 per cent of CPP/QPP and EI payments for the year. Both the employee contribution and the "employer" amount that self-employed persons contribute to the CPP/QPP have been converted from a deduction to a credit.

For 1998, the EI premium rate for employees is $2.70 per $100 of income up to a maximum of $39,000 of income. Maximum

EI contributions are $1,474.20 for employers and $1,053 for employees. The ceiling for 1998 earnings under CPP is $36,900, an increase of $1,100 over 1997. The maximum CPP payment is $1,068.80 by each of the employer and employee, based on a contribution rate of 3.2 per cent.

A self-employed person is not eligible for EI benefits, and therefore does not have to make contributions. Self-employed individuals must make CPP contributions, however, and the maximum contribution was increased to $2,137.60 for 1998, based on a contribution rate of 6.4 per cent.

NEW **New for 1998!** Employers who hire individuals between the ages of 18 and 24 during both 1999 and 2000 are not required to pay EI premiums for those individuals in those two years.

Expenses Connected with Employment—The General Rules

Generally, employees are not entitled to claim deductions for expenditures they incur as a result of their employment, unless these deductions are specifically authorized in the *Income Tax Act*.

Deductible Expenses

Employment expenses that may be deductible include: union or professional dues (not including the initiation fee); automobile expenses—if you use your own automobile for your employer's business, or in your own business, you may be entitled to deduct automobile expenses (see also Chapter 15); moving expenses (discussed below); and supplies consumed in the performance of your duties, if you are required by contract to pay for them (the courts have interpreted "supplies consumed in the performance of your duties" quite narrowly). Legal expenses incurred to collect or establish a right to salary or wages owing by an employer, or paid after 1985 to collect or establish a right to a retiring allowance (which includes awards for wrongful dismissal) or pension benefit, may also be deductible. The deduction is limited to the amounts received that are not transferred to an RRSP or

RPP. Excess amounts can be carried forward for deduction in any of the seven following years. Any reimbursement of these fees must be included in income.

You are also allowed to deduct the costs of care provided by a part-time attendant, who is not the individual's spouse or a person under the age of 18, for an individual certified as having a severe and prolonged impairment. There is no maximum amount that may be deducted; however, it is limited to two-thirds of eligible income, which includes income from employment or self-employment, or a grant for research or similar work (net of expenses). This deduction is in addition to the personal tax credit (mental or physical impairment) that may be claimed by such a certified person.

Special expense deduction provisions are provided for clergy, travelling salespeople, musicians, artists, and certain railway and transport employees. If you qualify, be sure you have the appropriate prescribed forms signed by your employer.

Moving Expenses

Moving expenses are deductible if you meet certain conditions and the expenses are not reimbursed by your employer. The moving expenses must be incurred in connection with beginning a business, employment, or full-time post-secondary education at a new location. The distance between your old residence and your new work or school location must be at least 40 kilometres greater than the distance between your new residence and your new work or school location.

Qualifying expenditures include the travelling costs to move you, your family, and your household goods, as well as meals and lodging en route, disposal costs in respect of your old residence, and legal services in respect of the purchase of the new residence, provided you or your spouse sold your old residence. You also may deduct storage costs for your household goods that are incurred in the course of the move. For 1998 and later years, moving expenses include certain expenses in connection with maintaining a vacant former residence, subject to certain maximums of amounts and time. There are limits on the total amount that will be deductible, depending on the particular circumstances of your move. Remember that you must be earning taxable income in your new location to claim the deduction.

Remote Work Locations, Special Work Sites, and Northern Residents Deductions

These three deductions are closely related, particularly in the employment context, but each has specific qualification criteria.

Remote Work Location Deduction. There are two categories of criteria to be satisfied before this deduction can be claimed. A remote work location is one that is 30 kilometres or more from the nearest community of at least 40,000 people and that lacks essential services (medical and educational facilities, housing, and food shopping). The employee must be working in the remote work location for longer than 36 hours because of work commitments. Overall, the conditions must be such that the employee could not reasonably be expected to set up and maintain a self-contained dwelling unit.

When employees are eligible for benefits for remote work locations, they can exclude from their income allowances for (or the value of) free or subsidized housing, board and certain transportation.

Special Work Site Deduction. If an employee is undertaking temporary work for an employer far enough away from his or her principal residence that it is not reasonable to expect the employee to commute daily, the employee may qualify under this deduction. The 36-hour requirement also applies here and the benefits to the employee are the same as for the remote site deduction. Employees and their employers must complete a *Declaration of Exemption—Employment at Special Work Sites* form before the employers can exclude the relevant benefits or allowances from the employees' income.

Northern Residents Deduction. If an individual resides within a northern Canadian area designated by Revenue Canada on a permanent basis for at least six months, he or she may qualify to claim the northern residents deduction. This deduction consists of two deductions: a residency deduction and a deduction for travel benefits received from an employer in the designated area. Revenue Canada has set the residency deduction at a ceiling based on the lesser of two amounts: 20 per cent of net income for the year, or a $7.50 per day basic residency amount for every day the individual lived in the designated area and an additional $7.50 per day for each day the individual maintained a self-contained dwelling unit and no other occupant of the dwelling claimed the basic deduction. The maximum amount that may be claimed is $5,475 per year. The deduction for travel relates to the value of two employer-provided trips per year and unlimited amounts for travel for medical reasons.

Deduction Available for Imputed Interest

Employees may claim an offsetting deduction for any imputed interest included in income as a taxable benefit arising from an employee loan, provided that the interest would otherwise be deductible if it had been actually paid. For example, low-interest or interest-free loans used for investment purposes (including investment in shares of an employer corporation) or for the purchase of an automobile or aircraft used in the business of the employer would qualify. (You will want to consider the tax treatment of automobiles used for business purposes, discussed in Chapter 15.)

Any potential deduction is available only to the debtor, even though the interest benefit may be included in another taxpayer's (i.e., the employee's) income. Where there is a potential interest deduction, it is recommended that the employee be the debtor; otherwise, the employee will have the taxable benefit but not the offsetting deduction. If the debtor is in a higher tax bracket than the employee, it would be an advantage for the deduction to be in the hands of the debtor.

PLANNING OPPORTUNITIES

Benefits from Employee Loans

Interest-free or low-interest loans can produce a worthwhile benefit even if interest is imputed as a taxable benefit, because the tax on the imputed interest would always be less than the interest paid in the marketplace. If you borrow $25,000 from your employer at 6 per cent and otherwise would have to borrow at 8 per cent, you will save $500 each year in interest charges. No taxable benefit arises because the rate of interest you pay is higher than or equal to the prescribed rate (assuming that the prescribed rate does not exceed 6 per cent). Note that the interest would have to be paid by January 30 of the following year or it would not reduce the imputed benefit.

Of course, the benefits are even greater if the employee loan is interest-free. If your marginal rate of tax is 44 per cent and you borrow $25,000, your cost of the loan is the tax paid on the imputed benefit of $1,500 ($25,000 at 6 per cent), which is $660 (assuming the prescribed rate is 6 per cent throughout the year and the loan is outstanding for a full year). This works out to an effective interest charge of 2.64 per cent and a saving of $1,340, compared to the 8 per cent loan ($2,000 minus $660). If the loan is used to earn investment income, the imputed interest of $1,500 is deductible and there is no cost associated with the loan, whereas your after-tax cost on a conventional loan would be $1,120 ($2,000 less tax saving at 44 per cent).

Common Income Deferral Strategies

Deferred Income Plans. Employers frequently offer such plans, many of which involve retirement planning. Whether tax is deferred on employment income depends on the nature of your particular plan.

Employee Stock Options. The tax rules relating to stock options are extremely complex. To avoid any nasty tax surprises, it would be best to obtain professional advice on this subject.

Retiring Allowances. To a certain extent, a retiring allowance can be considered a means of deferring income. It must not take the form of a deferred salary, however, which would be the case if an employee accepted a relatively low salary in exchange for a generous so-called "retiring allowance."

A retiring allowance is an amount (other than a superannuation or pension benefit or an amount received as a consequence of the death of an employee) received by the employee on or after retirement in recognition of long service. It includes early retirement incentives or any payment received in respect of a loss of employment, whether or not received as a termination payment or damages from loss of office. Termination payments are fully taxable, although tax may be deferred by transferring eligible amounts to an RRSP.

A retiring allowance may be received by your dependant or relative after your death or by your estate, and tax may also be deferred by transferring eligible amounts to an RRSP.

Recent legislative amendments limit the ability of employees to transfer only those retiring allowance payments that relate to years of service before 1996. The maximum amount of a retiring allowance that can be transferred on a tax-free basis to a registered pension plan or RRSP is $2,000 for each calendar year before 1996 that the employee was employed by the employer paying the amount. If the employee was not a member of the employer's pension plan or deferred profit sharing plan (DPSP), an additional $1,500 may be transferred to a registered pension plan or an RRSP for each year that the employee was employed by the employer prior to 1988. Eligible amounts may still be transferred after 1995, but the years after 1995 cannot be included in the calculation.

Any amount of a retiring allowance not transferred to either a registered pension plan or RRSP must be included in income in the year it is received and will be taxed at your marginal rate.

NEW **New for 1998!** The Alternative Minimum Tax no longer applies to amounts paid into an RRSP, including retiring allowances that are transferred. This will be retroactive to 1994.

For Quebec tax purposes, since 1997, the retiring allowance transferred to an RRSP is not taken into consideration in calculating the Quebec Alternative Minimum Tax.

A retiring allowance cannot be transferred to a spousal RRSP.

Planning Opportunity: You can arrange for your employer to transfer your retiring allowance directly to your RRSP, in which case no tax need be withheld.

If you receive the amount directly from your employer and then make the transfer, your employer must withhold tax. You can then claim the tax as tax withheld during the year in your next return, and it will increase your refund or decrease your balance of tax owing.

Contributions to Deferred Profit Sharing Plans (DPSPs).
Your employer may be making deductible contributions to a DPSP on your behalf. The maximum employer contribution for the years 1998 to 2002 will be limited to the lesser of 18 per cent of the employee's remuneration or $6,750, and will increase to $7,250 in 2003 and $7,750 in 2004.

Caution: The amount contributed on your behalf by your employer will reduce the amount that you may contribute to your RRSP in the next year.

The maximum figure will be indexed beginning in 2005 according to increases in the average wage. DPSPs must provide that the employer make a contribution based on company profits, but no contribution need be made in a loss year. A DPSP does not permit any type of past service contribution or employee contribution.

Proceeds from DPSPs. Amounts received from DPSPs must be included in income, except for capital amounts contributed by the employee for the years in which such contributions were permitted by law. Most plans allow for payment of taxable amounts to be spread over a maximum of 10 years. Otherwise, it is possible before reaching age 69 to purchase an annuity for life, although, if there are guaranteed terms, they cannot exceed 15 years. Employee contributions may be withdrawn at any time. DPSP proceeds can also be deferred by transferring them into a registered pension plan, an RRSP, or another eligible DPSP. This must be done by the time the taxpayer turns 69 (as of 1997).

If the DPSP was previously an employee profit sharing plan at any time in the past, you are entitled to exclude an additional amount from income.

Salary Deferral Arrangements (SDAs). The rules concerning SDAs were introduced to prevent abuses prevalent with respect to employee benefit plans.

An SDA is defined as a funded or unfunded plan between an employee and employer under which the employee has postponed the receipt of his or her remuneration beyond the end of a year. The rules restrict the ability of employees to defer the tax payable on salary earned by him or her in the year or a preceding year.

A variety of plans are excluded from the definition, including registered pension plans and other registered plans, certain benefit plans such as group sickness or accident insurance plans, plans to defer the salary of certain professional athletes, plans to provide funds for the education of workers, three-year bonus plans, and self-funded leave of absence plans.

In limited circumstances, the rules regarding SDAs do not apply to plans that existed before February 26, 1986.

Under the SDA rules, a right to receive deferred amounts, whether funded or not, must be recognized for tax purposes as it is accrued, meaning that it must be included in the employment income of the employee in the year the amount is earned, even if not yet received. The employer will receive a deduction for the amount in that year. Interest or other amounts paid by the employer in respect of the deferred salary will be treated as employment income in the year earned and not necessarily in the year it is received. If a person other than the employee has a right to receive the deferred salary, these rules still apply.

Retirement Compensation Arrangements (RCAs). An RCA is any plan or arrangement established after October 8, 1986, under which payments are made by an employer or former employer (or related person) of a taxpayer to a custodian. These payments must relate to benefits that will be provided to the taxpayer or others on the retirement, loss of office, etc., of the taxpayer. Certain arrangements are specifically excluded from the definition, such as registered pension plans, employee profit sharing plans and DPSPs, RRSPs, group sickness and accident insurance plans, certain plans established for professional athletes and officials, and SDAs.

Contributions to an RCA are deductible by the employer when made, but are subject to a refundable 50 per cent withholding tax (except for Quebec tax purposes). This tax is refunded when payments are made from the RCA and included in the recipient's income. Income earned in the RCA on the contributions is also subject to a 50 per cent tax that is refundable when payments are made to beneficiaries. Any income from an RCA is not taxable to the recipient until actually received. An employee may make contributions to an RCA, which are deductible by him or her, but these contributions are also subject to the 50 per cent refundable tax.

Employee Benefit Plans (EBPs). In the unlikely event that a deferral plan does not fall within the definition of an SDA or an

RCA, the plan likely is an EBP. In this case, the employer will not receive a deduction for amounts deferred. Prior to the introduction of the SDA rules, EBPs were frequently used to defer the salary of employees who worked for non-taxable employers, such as government, non-profit organizations, or companies in a loss position.

Under an EBP, a portion of the employee's salary is placed with a custodian. The employer receives no deduction for amounts directed to the custodian, and the employee is not taxed on these amounts until they are actually received. Investment income earned on the deferred amounts is taxed in the hands of the plan, or in the hands of the employee or employer.

In a self-funded leave of absence arrangement, under which an employee may defer up to one-third of his or her salary each year for up to six years, the deferred amount must be included in the employee's income for tax purposes in the seventh year. The total deferred amount must be included to the extent it has not previously been received and included in income.

Unpaid Remuneration. Deferring remuneration provides only a limited benefit. An employer is not allowed a deduction for remuneration expense in the year incurred if the amount remains unpaid to the employee for more than 179 days after the year-end of the employer. The employer will receive the deduction in the year the remuneration is actually paid. This provision applies whether or not the employer and employee are related. Remuneration expense does not include reasonable amounts for vacation or holiday pay, or deferred amounts under an SDA.

The SDA rules do not affect remuneration amounts paid within the 180-day limit. Thus, for the year the remuneration is earned, employees will not have to include a benefit in income for tax purposes equal to the unpaid amount.

Shareholder Loans

If you are a shareholder as well as an employee, you should consider the special rules regarding loans or advances from your company. Although many of the rules for low-interest and interest-free loans are the same, there are greater tax implications regarding the granting of shareholder loans.

If a shareholder or a person related to the shareholder receives a loan or incurs any type of indebtedness from the shareholder's corporation or a related corporation, and the amount is not repaid by the end of the lender's following taxation year, the amount of the loan is included in the debtor's income in the year the loan was made. Depending on the corporation's year-end in relation to the taxpayer's year-end (the calendar year), the taxpayer may be required to amend his or her income tax return. If the amount is included in income and is repaid at a later date, it is deductible from income in the year of repayment. A repayment that is a part of a series of loans and repayments would not qualify for the deduction.

In the year of repayment, you should ensure that you have sufficient income to absorb any deduction resulting from the repayment of such a loan. This is necessary, since if the amount of the repayment exceeds other income, the excess will be a non-capital loss that can be carried back.

There are four other exceptions to the rules requiring a loan to be included in income:

- when the creditor lends the money as part of its ordinary business;
- when loans are made to employees of the creditor or their spouses, enabling the employee or spouse to purchase a dwelling for their own habitation;
- when loans are made to employees of the creditor, enabling the employee to purchase an automobile for employment purposes;
- when a corporate creditor lends funds to employees, enabling the employees to purchase, from the corporation or a related corporation, fully paid treasury shares of the corporation for their own benefit.

This last provision does not provide for the employee to purchase shares from any other shareholder; rather, they must be purchased directly from the corporation. In each of the four cases above, bona fide arrangements for repayment of the loan or indebtedness within a reasonable period must be in place at the time the loan is made.

A loan made to an employee who is a shareholder must be made to him or her as an employee, and not as a shareholder, in order for the exemptions to apply. Accordingly, the loan would have to be available to all employees. The effect of this requirement is that the exclusion is denied to loans made by a company in which all the employees are also shareholders.

The taxable benefit rules regarding imputed interest on low-interest or interest-free employee loans apply for the most part to all types of shareholder loans and indebtedness (see above). The home purchase and home relocation loan rules don't apply to shareholder loans unless the shareholder is an employee and the loan was received because of the borrower's status as an employee.

Advances to shareholders during the year in anticipation of dividend payments are considered to be indebtedness, and the imputed interest taxable benefit rules apply.

The act under which a corporation was formed may contain restrictions on lending money to employees, officers, directors, and shareholders of the corporation. Reference should be made to the act before any such loan is made.

CHAPTER EIGHT

If You Are a Business Owner

IF YOU ARE A SOLE PROPRIETOR OR IN A PARTNERSHIP

Income from a Business Defined

The category of business income is fairly broad. If an activity is a business, you are taxed on the "profit" from that business. Profit is calculated by deducting the expenses incurred in generating revenue from the total revenue earned. As a sole proprietor, you declare your profit in your personal tax return. If you realize a loss on the activity, this loss may offset income from other sources, including employment and investment income. (If the losses are generated from farming, restrictions exist preventing you from using them to offset other types of income, including income from other businesses.)

If the income or a portion of it is derived from the sale or transfer of property, it could be characterized by Revenue Canada either as business income or income from property. If it is characterized as business income, it will be fully included in calculating taxable income. If it is considered income from property, the proceeds of the sale or transfer will be a capital gain, eligible for a partial exclusion.

The economic reality of the activity should control its tax treatment. However, it is absolutely critical that you have detailed documentation of your activity.

If you are starting a new business while you remain employed, you must maintain detailed records to demonstrate that you have a reasonable expectation of profit from the business, and that you are approaching the business in a professional manner. This includes obtaining businesslike advice, if necessary, and demonstrating that you either have abilities in the field or are seeking guidance. If you cannot demonstrate an expectation of profit and a businesslike approach to the activity, you may be treated as having a hobby. If so, your tax deductions will be restricted to the income generated from the activity. If the activity generates a loss, you will not be able to offset the loss against other income. Maintaining such records is particularly important for any activity, including part-time farming. If your activity generates losses for a number of years, Revenue Canada is strongly inclined to view it as a hobby rather than a business.

If you have entered into the activity as an investment, hoping to use the property acquired to generate income, it is equally important that you document this intent and provide evidence that it is reasonable to expect that the property will give rise to investment income. For example, if you buy a piece of land, expecting to build an office building or some other income-generating asset, the land may be a capital asset eligible for capital gains treatment on disposition. On the other hand, if you invest in land with the intention of holding it to generate income from its rise in value, this action would probably be considered an adventure in the nature of trade, or a business (depending on the volume of similar activity), and any profit would probably be fully taxable income. (Revenue Canada is more inclined to treat increases in value as ordinary income and decreases in value as capital than they are to treat increases as capital and decreases as ordinary income.)

Taxation of Income from a Business

There are numerous opportunities for tax planning if you are self-employed or own a business because of the different tax rules that apply to business income. Taxation of income from your business will differ depending on whether the business is operated in corporate or unincorporated form. The second part of this chapter discusses the advantages and disadvantages of incorporation, as well as a number of aspects of tax planning for small incorporated businesses. If you are considering incorporating your small business, you can transfer assets from an unincorporated business to a partnership or a corporation on a tax-deferred basis, subject to certain restrictions.

Overall, you will be taxed on the "profit" from your business, regardless of how much you withdraw from the business (assuming your business is unincorporated). Profit is measured by deducting from the gross income of the business the various expenses that are allowed as deductions. These expenses must be reasonable in amount and must be incurred for the purpose of generating income. Common deductions include the cost of merchandise sold, and expenditures for salaries, supplies, rent, advertising, and so forth. The amounts spent for items such as furniture or equipment are not deductible, but you may claim capital cost allowances (depreciation) for such acquisitions.

Except for farming and fishing, profit is determined on an accrual basis, rather than on a cash basis.

Taxation Year

Unincorporated businesses are required to operate with a December 31 fiscal year-end. Except for certain professional partnerships, an unincorporated business may have any year-end, but it must adjust its income from the business to a calendar year for tax purposes. Individuals and eligible partnerships that initially adopt an off-calendar fiscal year-end are permitted to change to a December 31 fiscal year-end for a taxation year. They are required, though, to provide notification before the filing deadline for the individuals' or partners' income tax returns for the year of the change. Once a business of an individual or eligible partnership has adopted a December 31 fiscal year-end, it cannot subsequently change to an off-calendar fiscal year-end.

DEDUCTIONS

Home Office Expenses

If you are self-employed or run your own sideline business and have an office in your home, you may be able to deduct expenses relating to that office.

⚠ **Caution:** For home office expenses to be deductible, the office must be your principal place of business, or must be used exclusively to earn business income and be used on a regular and continuous basis for meeting clients, customers, or patients.

The amount deducted cannot exceed the income from the business for the year, after other expenses are deducted. Any excess amount may be carried forward to be deducted in years when the business generates income. In Quebec, home office expenses are limited to 50 per cent of the amount that would otherwise be deductible.

Deductible Interest

If you borrow funds to earn income, see the section "Deductible Interest" in Chapter 9.

The Facts on Golf and Entertainment Expenses

NEW **New for 1998!** Expenses incurred for the use of a golf course are not deductible, but meals will qualify for the 50 per cent deduction, provided that certain restrictions are satisfied. Federal legislation precludes claims for both annual club membership dues and green fees, even in cases where belonging to a golf club and organizing golf tournaments with clients, suppliers, or staff are justified by business reasons. Meals and beverages consumed at a golf course or club's dining rooms, banquet halls, conference rooms, and lounges are deductible as entertainment expenses provided there is a genuine business purpose to the use of the facilities. The meal and beverage expenses must be clearly itemized to qualify for the deduction. If the purpose of the golf club expenses relates to a charity fundraiser or an office golf day, the expenses are 100 per cent deductible. The Quebec government has adopted a similar position.

Deduction for Private Health Service Plan Contributions

NEW **New for 1998!** If you are self-employed, you are now eligible to deduct premiums and contributions to private health service plans (PHSPs) from your business income. Eligible plans, covering medical and dental services, may be for the benefit of you and your immediate family.

A self-employed individual is defined as an individual actively engaged in business alone or with a partner. Your business must be your primary source of income or your income from other sources must not exceed $10,000 for the year.

The maximum amount deductible is $1,500 for you and your spouse and $750 for each of your children. If you claim a deduction under this credit, you cannot also claim the medical expenses credit for the same expenditure.

If you hire full-time employees for your business, you must offer equivalent coverage to all of them. The deduction limits will not apply if more than one-half of your full-time employees are covered under the PHSP.

PLANNING OPPORTUNITY

Hiring Your Spouse and Children

Provided you can establish that your spouse and/or children earn income for the business in some fashion, you can split income with them by paying them a salary. The salary must be reasonable in light of the duties performed.

IF YOU HAVE AN INCORPORATED BUSINESS

If you own your own business, you may wonder whether to incorporate or not. Traditionally, the Canadian income tax system has favoured incorporated Canadian small businesses. The calculations for income and deductions remain essentially the same as for an unincorporated business. There are some differences, however, in the structure of corporate taxation, and in planning opportunities through corporations. Tax planning for your business may provide opportunities for income splitting, tax deferral, increasing your capital gains exemption, estate planning, and retirement planning. Because these are complex tasks involving tax and corporate and family law issues, consult your professional tax advisor for personalized planning in this area.

Corporation Defined

A corporation is a completely separate legal entity from the shareholders or incorporators with the following characteristics:

- As a separate legal entity, it has an ongoing existence and the ability to enter into contracts (i.e., buy, sell, employ, borrow, loan, and own property).
- It must act through individuals.
- Ownership is represented by shareholders who may also be employees.
- Profits are distributed by dividends, which are taxed in the hands of the shareholders.
- It is a separate taxable entity and must file income tax returns and pay taxes.

Corporate Taxation: The Basics

If you run your business as a sole proprietorship, you include the income from the business on your personal tax return. A corporation, on the other hand, is a separate taxable entity. The corporation must file its own tax return and pay its own tax instalments. You include income from the corporation on your personal tax return only when you receive distributions from your corporation in the form of salary, dividends, interest, or some other payment.

Similar to the individual rate structure, the corporate structure varies based on the province where the corporate income is generated. In addition, however, the tax rate varies depending on the type and amount of income.

The basic federal income tax rate for corporations is 38 per cent. This rate is decreased to 28 per cent on income earned in Canada to accommodate provincial and territorial taxation on such income. A further deduction from the basic tax rate is available for income generated from manufacturing and processing activities (M&P) performed in Canada. The M&P deduction is 7 per cent, reducing the federal corporate rate to 21 per cent.

There is also a federal surtax of 4 per cent of the net federal rate, which increases the federal tax rate for income earned in a province from 28 per cent to 29.12 per cent without the M&P deduction, and to 22.12 per cent with the M&P deduction.

Canadian-Controlled Private Corporations (CCPCs)

A CCPC is a resident Canadian corporation, controlled by Canadian residents (other than public corporations). Generally, this control will exist if the Canadian residents hold at least 50 per cent of the voting rights in the company.

This is not always the case, however. When a person has any direct or indirect influence that, if exercised, would result in control of the corporation in fact, he or she is considered to have control of the corporation. For example, a person who holds 49 per cent of the votes of a corporation may be considered to control it where the balance of the votes is widely dispersed among employees of the corporation or is held by a person who could reasonably be considered to act in accordance with the wishes of the person holding the 49 per cent voting interest.

> **Planning Opportunity:** A CCPC is eligible for a federal tax rate reduction (the small business deduction—SBD) on up to $200,000 of active business income annually. (If the corporation's tax year is less than 12 months, this amount must be prorated.) The federal SBD is 16 per cent.

The federal tax rate reduction may apply to a lesser amount, or even be completely cancelled, if the capital of the corporation and associated corporations for the previous year exceeded $10 million.

The annual $200,000 limit must be shared by "associated corporations" to prevent taxpayers from abusing the SBD by forming several corporations to multiply the $200,000 eligible for the reduced rate. Generally, associated corporations are corporations controlled by the same person or group of persons. Because of this, it is not possible to set up several corporations and obtain the benefits of the SBD on $200,000 of income for each of them. Income, in this case, must be "active business income." If you incorporate your investment portfolio, you will not qualify for the SBD because the income generated will not be active business income.

There is no M&P deduction for income eligible for the SBD. Therefore, if your company is a CCPC generating income from an active business in Canada, the federal corporate tax rate will be 12 per cent for the first $200,000 of taxable income. When you include the 4 per cent federal surtax (calculated on 28 per cent), the federal income tax rate is 13.12 per cent. For income in excess of $200,000, the normal corporate tax rates apply.

In addition to the federal corporate tax, all provinces also impose income taxes. The provincial tax rates vary from nil to 17 per cent depending on the province, and depending on whether there is an M&P deduction, an SBD, and/or a tax holiday (often for new corporations). Combined federal and provincial corporate income tax rates, therefore, vary considerably.

Large Corporations

A federal tax is imposed at a rate of 0.225 per cent on a large corporation's capital employed in Canada in excess of $10 million. With such a large threshold, most small businesses are not subject to this large corporations tax (LCT). The 4 per cent surtax that corporations are required to pay can, however, be used to offset LCT liability. The LCT cannot be deducted in computing income subject to income tax.

Inherent Tax Deferral

For small companies, the combined federal-provincial corporate tax rate is between 18.12 and 23.12 per cent, depending on the province. In Quebec, a tax rate of 19.03 per cent is in effect for the 1998 calendar year. This will increase to 22.27 per cent on July 1, 1999. If you compare these rates to those for individuals (see Chapter 20), you'll notice that the small company rates are significantly lower.

If you operate your business in an unincorporated form, you will include the income from the business in your personal tax return as it is earned. Thus, you will pay tax on your business income at your personal marginal tax rate.

Planning Opportunity: If you incorporate your business, you initially pay only the corporate tax rate. You will not pay individual tax on the corporate earnings unless you receive distributions in the form of salary, interest, or dividends, and you are therefore able to defer the personal tax on the portion of earnings retained in the business.

For example, if you earned $1,000 of pre-tax income, you would pay about $530 in individual taxes at the top marginal rates. That would leave $470 for reinvestment in the business. If the $1,000 were generated by a corporation eligible for the SBD, the maximum corporate tax would be about $189, leaving $811 for reinvestment. No individual tax would be due until earnings were distributed to shareholders. In comparing the two, as much as $341 ($530 minus $189) of tax might be deferred.

Setting Up the Corporation

There are administrative costs associated with incorporating a business, resulting largely from the legal requirements of preparing and filing the appropriate documents with the government. Unlike other transfers of property, however, you can transfer your business assets to a corporation without any tax consequences, subject to certain restrictions. In return, the corporation must issue shares to you. You may choose to have part of your investment in the corporation in the form of debt rather than shares. By holding some debt, you have the opportunity to draw earnings out of the corporation as interest, which is tax-deductible to the company, as well as drawing earnings out as dividends.

Taxation of Distributions from the Corporation

When you receive payments from the corporation, the tax treatment depends on the nature of the payment. Salary you receive as an employee of your corporation is included in your income in the year of receipt. If you have financed your company partly by loaning the company money, any interest income is fully included in your income. If you have leased assets to the corporation, lease payments paid to you would be included in your income when received, and so forth.

All payments from the company to you are deductible in calculating the corporation's income. Deferring the tax on these payments is possible if you can obtain a tax deduction for the corporation before you have to pay the individual tax on the payments. There are some restrictions on deferring income that limit your ability to delay accrued payables.

It may be possible to achieve limited deferral through the payment of salaries or bonuses. In such cases, for the corporation to obtain a deduction in the year the salaries or bonuses were accrued, these amounts must be paid within 180 days after the corporation's year-end. When they are paid, you include them in your taxable income. However, if the corporate year-end is after July 5 (e.g., a July 31 year-end or later), the amounts can be paid in the following calendar year, but within 180 days after the corporation's year-end. This delay provides about six months of tax deferral benefit.

Integration

Although you may own most or all of the shares of a corporation, you and the corporation are separate taxpayers. The corporation pays its own income tax when it earns a profit. When the after-tax profits are distributed from the corporation as dividends, they are included in your income and the corporation does not receive a deduction. Consequently, profits generated through a corporation are taxed twice, once when earned by the corporation and again when distributed as dividends to the shareholders.

To alleviate this double taxation of income earned through a corporation, the corporate and individual tax systems are integrated. This integration is accomplished by grossing up the dividend received by the shareholder to approximate the amount earned before tax at the corporate level. A tax credit is then granted in an amount designed to give the shareholder a credit for the amount of tax already paid by the corporation.

Accordingly, when you calculate your total dividend income from the corporation, you gross up (increase) the dividend by 25 per cent of the dividend to calculate your total dividend income amount. After you calculate your federal income tax on the grossed-up amount (before calculating the surtax of 8 per cent), you take a dividend tax credit equal to two-thirds of the grossed-up portion of the dividend. For Quebec taxes, the dividend tax credit is 44 per cent of the dividend gross-up.

For example:

Dividend received	$100
Dividend gross-up (25% × $100)	25
Taxable income	$125
Federal tax at 29% (maximum)	$ 36.25
Dividend tax credit ($\frac{2}{3}$ × $25)	(16.67)
Federal tax before surtax	$ 19.58
Federal surtax (8% × $19.58)	1.57
Total federal tax	$ 21.15
Provincial tax (55% assumed rate × $19.58)	10.77
Total individual tax on dividend	$ 31.92

The integration system is rough justice designed to approximate an individual receiving dividends from a corporation that has already enjoyed the small business deduction. To achieve perfect integration, the federal and provincial combined corporate rate must be 20 per cent, with no surtaxes, and the individual must have a provincial tax rate of 50 per cent. Under these conditions, there will be no difference between earning business income through a corporation or directly, as demonstrated in the following example (assuming the taxpayer is in the highest tax bracket).

How Tax Integration Works for Individuals in the Highest Tax Bracket

	Income Earned Directly	Income Earned Through a Corporation
Corporate income		$100
Corporate tax		20
After-tax profits		$ 80
Individual income:		
Business profits	$100	
Dividend		$ 80
Dividend gross-up (25% × $80)		20
Taxable income	$100	$100
Federal tax at 29%	$ 29	$ 29
Dividend tax credit (⅔ × $20)	0	(13.33)
Provincial tax at 50%	14.50	7.83
Total individual tax	43.50	23.50
Corporate tax	0	20.00
Total tax on $100 income	$ 43.50	$ 43.50

To the extent that the tax rates differ from these hypothetical rates, there will be differences in total taxes paid depending on whether the income is earned directly by an individual or through a corporation. If the corporate tax rate and/or individual tax rates are lower than these hypothetical rates, the total tax paid on income earned through the corporate structure is likely to be less than the total tax that would be paid if the income were earned directly by the individual. To the extent that the corporate tax rates are higher than for a small business corporation, there will be a shortfall in relief from double taxation.

Advantages and Disadvantages of Incorporating Your Business

To a great extent, the trade-offs between the corporate and unincorporated structures depend on the nature of your activities and the income generated. Either mode favours a range of activity type and scale. Compare the corporate and individual tax rates for the province in which you do business to determine how much of a tax difference exists between the two rates. From a purely tax standpoint, in many cases it will be advantageous to have a corporate structure.

Generally, the tax and non-tax advantages to incorporating your business include:

- *Limited Liability.* Because the corporation is a separate legal entity, individual shareholders are not responsible for corporate debts or other liabilities. This may not apply to a small business because it is common for lending institutions to request personal guarantees on loans to such a corporation. Your liability remains limited for such things as lawsuits, however, unless you are personally negligent.
- *Tax Savings or Deferral.* As mentioned above, there may be tax-saving opportunities and tax-deferral opportunities. The saving or deferral opportunities are of particular value to a business that will be investing to expand. The extent of these opportunities depends on the comparative corporate and individual tax rates in the particular circumstances, as well as on the nature of the income earned.

- *Income Splitting and Estate Planning*. There are income splitting and estate planning opportunities available through a corporate structure that are not available with an unincorporated business.
- *Levelling of Income*. It is possible to achieve a levelling of personal income through control of salary and dividends to avoid high- and low-income periods, particularly in a business where profits fluctuate from year to year.
- *Pension Plans*. A shareholder who is also an employee of the corporation may participate in the company's registered pension plan (RPP). A sole proprietor may not participate in an RPP. There also are other types of fringe benefits such as group term life insurance plans and group sickness or accident insurance plans, which may be available to you as an employee of your company, but are not available if your business is unincorporated.
- *Capital Gains Exemption*. The corporate structure permits access to the capital gains exemption on the sale of shares of the corporation running the business. The $500,000 capital gains exemption is available to holders of shares of a small business corporation (it is not available if the business is unincorporated). This exemption includes the regular $100,000 capital gains exemption on other capital properties, which was abolished on February 22, 1994.

  To qualify for the $500,000 exemption, the corporation must be a small business corporation at the time of the sale and the shares must not have been held by anyone other than the seller, or related persons, within the 24 months preceding the sale. In addition, throughout the 24-month period, more than 50 per cent of the fair market value of the assets of the corporation must be used in an active business carried on primarily in Canada. A "small business corporation" is a CCPC provided that it uses all or substantially all (90 per cent or more, expressed in terms of fair market value, according to Revenue Canada) of the fair market value of its assets in an active business carried on primarily in Canada. The shares of a Canadian holding company also qualify if substantially all of its assets are shares or debt of other small business corporations.

Disadvantages of the corporate structure include:

- *Losses.* A corporation is unable to use losses to offset income generated by the individual. If you generate losses through an unincorporated business, you may use these losses to offset income from other activities. Because the corporation is a separate entity, neither the income nor the losses flow directly to your individual tax return. As a result, you cannot use these losses to offset other types of income. If the corporation generates income in other years, the losses may offset such other income of the corporation. Specifically, business losses of the corporation for a given year may be carried back three years and forward seven years to offset other income of the corporation. If your corporation is generating a loss, the reported loss can be adjusted by reducing your salary payments and substituting dividends.
- *Costs of Incorporating.* There are additional costs to setting up and maintaining a corporation that you would not attract with an unincorporated business. Such costs include the initial expenses of preparing the legal documents as well as added taxes such as provincial capital taxes. Ongoing costs include those associated with filing forms such as tax returns, holding meetings, maintaining corporate records, and so forth.
- *Capital Taxes.* In 1989, the federal government introduced a special tax similar to the capital tax system that has existed in some provinces for years. Because this tax is payable only when the capital used in Canada by the corporation exceeds $10 million, the federal capital tax liability is usually eliminated or substantially reduced for small corporations.

  The Quebec capital tax rate is 0.64 per cent. An exemption is available for the first three taxation years of a newly incorporated business with paid-up capital less than $2 million. Nevertheless, a minimum capital tax of $250 must be paid each year.

PLANNING OPPORTUNITIES

In addition to tax-planning opportunities, it is also important to keep in mind non-tax factors while developing your plan for your business. You must consider your cash needs, and the cash needs of the company. In addition, you must review all other sources of income, and your position regarding investment income, capital gains, and investment losses. All of these factors should be considered when you are reviewing your tax planning for your company.

Payment of Investment Income

One aspect you may want to review is your position under the cumulative net investment loss (CNIL) rules (see also Chapter 9). In short, these apply if you have not earned sufficient investment income to cover your claimed investment expenses or losses. An outstanding CNIL will prevent you from claiming the $500,000 capital gains exemption on the proceeds of sale of otherwise qualifying capital property.

If you have outstanding CNILs, one common strategy for reducing them is to be paid in the form of interest or dividend income from your corporation. This income would be netted against any investment losses to reduce the amount of your CNIL, thereby regaining room to claim any available capital gains exemption once your CNIL amount reaches zero.

Spousal Salaries

As with an unincorporated business, you can pay a salary to your spouse or other family members. It is necessary that the person actually perform some services for the company, that there be a bona fide employer-employee relationship, and that you be able to support the salary as reasonable. A salary generally will be considered reasonable if a reasonable businessperson would have paid the salary under similar circumstances and the amount is commensurate with the value of the responsibilities assumed and the services performed.

Under these conditions, the corporation will obtain a deduction for the salary payment, and you will have achieved additional income splitting. This salary payment also may create an opportunity for increased contributions to retirement savings plans for that family member. By earning income, your spouse will create more room for contributions to a registered retirement savings plan (RRSP).

Salary/Dividend Trade-Offs

One of the interesting areas of planning for the owner-managed corporation is the determination of the appropriate split between salary payments and dividend payments for the owner-manager.

Salary reduces corporate income tax payable, but the salary is subject to personal tax. Although a dividend does not reduce corporate tax, the dividend tax credit means less personal tax is paid than on salary income. In theory, it is not supposed to matter whether you draw a salary or a dividend provided the company's taxable income (and that of all associated companies, prorated for any tax years less than 12 months) is not more than $200,000.

As with integration, this theory is effective only when the combined federal and provincial corporate rate is 20 per cent, there are no surtaxes, and the individual is in a 29 per cent federal tax bracket in a province imposing tax at 50 per cent of the federal rate. In such a case, if 100 per cent of after-tax corporate income is distributed, the total tax would be identical whether it is distributed as salary or dividends. (For every $100 of corporate income the numbers would be identical to the previous example.)

The theory is fine, but the system does not work exactly in the way it was intended. While in many provinces drawing a salary and maximizing RRSP contributions will be preferable to drawing a dividend, this is not true for all provinces, nor for all types of business activities.

....

✓ **Planning Opportunity:** As the main corporate owner, your best plan is to withdraw from the company an amount up to or equal to the level at which the net amount of tax you pay is equal to the tax the company would have paid had you not withdrawn the funds.

....

Depending on your particular circumstances, the most feasible way to do this may be taking all salary, or a combination of salary and dividends. If cash flow for the corporation is an issue, you can lend funds back to the company, and at any time in the future the company can repay the loan to you on a tax-free basis. Structuring your income using salary and dividends works if the corporation (and all associated companies, etc.) generates active business income of $200,000 or less, making its income eligible for the SBD.

If there is taxable income in the corporation in excess of $200,000, the SBD will not apply to this excess, and the corporate tax rate will be considerably higher. In light of this, it is advisable to keep the taxable income of the corporate group at or below $200,000. If the income of your corporation or corporate group is near the threshold, the most common way of achieving this goal is through salary payments to you as the owner-manager.

Remember that this salary will be included in your taxable income in the year of receipt. Depending on the timing of salary payments, the corporation might receive a deduction for your salary in the year before you actually receive it. There may be a slight deferral advantage to leaving income in the corporation, but the total tax is likely to be higher than if salaries were paid.

From a personal tax perspective, it is important to maximize the amounts that you can contribute under the Canada/Quebec Pension Plan and RRSPs. These plans have contribution limits based on your earned income for the year. As a result, even though the corporate income may be less than $200,000 without additional salaries or bonuses, you may want to pay enough salary to yourself to maximize your contributions to such plans, providing you have not fully used your pension amount in a company pension plan.

The contribution limit for RRSPs for a given year is based on the income earned in the preceding year. Consequently, your earned income in the preceding year must be at least $75,000 to contribute the maximum amount ($13,500) to your RRSP for the current year.

For salaries to be deductible by the corporation, they must be "reasonable." What constitutes a reasonable salary is generally a question of fact. As a rule, however, Revenue Canada will not question the payment of a salary or bonus to a shareholder manager provided payroll tax withholdings are paid.

Selling Your Business

If your business is unincorporated, and you are contemplating its sale, you can in most cases transfer the assets to a corporation and then immediately sell the shares of the corporation to take advantage of the $500,000 capital gains exemption.

Purification. If your business is already incorporated, but does not qualify as a small business corporation, it may be possible to "purify" (i.e., ensure that it qualifies) the corporation by removing non-qualified assets from the company. With careful planning, this removal could be effected on a tax-free basis. The purification process should begin long before a sale is being contemplated. The *Income Tax Act* contains provisions that may deny the transfer of such non-qualified assets on a tax-free basis, when the transfer occurs as part of the sale process.

Increasing Your Capital Gain. If you are expecting to sell the shares of your company, you could consider accumulating income in the company to increase the gain. This must be done carefully because, to maintain the small business corporation status, substantially all (90 per cent or more, according to Revenue Canada) of the assets, expressed in terms of fair market value, must be used in carrying on the corporation's business. As a result, you cannot accumulate earnings in the corporation and use those earnings to buy passive investments if such investments constitute more than 10 per cent of the total fair market value of the corporate assets at the time of sale (or more than 50 per cent for the preceding 24 months). Consider using the earnings to reduce the corporation's debts and other liabilities.

Buyer's Interest versus Vendor's Interest. When you are negotiating the sale of your business, the buyer may prefer to buy the assets of the company, rather than to buy your shares. This provides the buyer with tax write-offs that would be unavailable if the buyer purchased the shares. On the vendor's part, the preference will be for a sale of the shares. Profit on a sale of shares can be reduced by the capital gains exemption. In addition, if you previously have organized the share structure to permit ownership by your spouse and children, the exemption can also be claimed by them.

There is room for negotiation. If the disposition qualifies for the $500,000 capital gains exemption, negotiate a deal with a purchaser that permits both of you to share the tax benefits from your expanded capital gains exemption.

Corporate Planning and Your Family

It may be possible to reorganize the capital structure of your company to permit ownership by your spouse and children. A reorganization of the capital structure may provide both income splitting and estate planning opportunities if it is properly planned. Arranging for share ownership by a spouse and children also could provide for a reduction in tax if the company is sold. Specifically, if the corporation is a small business corporation, each family member would be entitled to the $500,000 capital gains exemption if the company is sold.

Reorganizing share capital does have its pitfalls and you should not proceed without proper advice.

CHAPTER NINE

....

If You Own Investments

INCOME FROM CAPITAL PROPERTY

The Basics

Income from capital property comes in the form of interest, dividends and capital gains. You will find more about interest and dividends later in this chapter. A capital gain or loss will occur when, upon the disposition (i.e., sale or transfer) of capital property, there is a difference between the owner's cost base of the property and the proceeds of disposition. Capital property is a broad category, but can generally be described as property that can appreciate (or depreciate, as the case may be) and that is generally held for the purpose of earning income.

The *Income Tax Act* creates numerous classes of capital property, including "personal use property," "listed personal property," "qualified small business corporation (generally CCPC) shares," "eligible capital property" (see "Special Cases," below), "flow-through entities" (see "Special Cases," below), and "other" depreciable properties in both tangible and intangible forms. These are defined terms in the Act and there are special rules regarding their disposition, valuation, and exemption of accrued gains. While we discuss some issues related to these classes of capital property, we focus on the category of "other" capital property. This "catch-all" class includes publicly traded shares, a common capital investment of Canadians. You should speak to your tax planning professional for issues relating to the other forms of capital property.

Capital gains first became taxable after December 31, 1971. That date is commonly referred to as the valuation date for all capital property. If you have owned capital property since before 1972 and plan to sell it, you must obtain the value of that property as of that date. The December 31, 1971, value will act as your cost base for the property for tax purposes.

If a sale of capital property results in the owner recognizing a gain, he or she must include three-quarters of that gain in taxable income for that year. If the owner loses money, three-quarters of the loss can be applied against current-year capital gains. If losses of other capital property exceed capital gains for a given year, the losses can be carried back three years and forward indefinitely and applied against capital gains.

Capital Gains Exemptions

The $100,000 capital gains exemption was abolished as of February 22, 1994. For individuals who had not exhausted their deduction, an election was allowed with 1994 income tax returns and special rules were created for the cancellation, amendment or late filing of an election.

The good news is that the $500,000 capital gains exemption for "qualified small business corporation shares" and "qualified farm property" is still available.

The $100,000 Capital Gains Exemption
The Effect of Making an Election on Capital Property.
An election made for capital property owned on February 22, 1994, created a deemed disposition and reacquisition of that property. The proceeds of the deemed disposition and the reacquisition amount were the same amounts (except for non-qualifying real property as discussed below) and the amount was designated by the owner. The designated amount could not exceed the property's fair market value at February 22, 1994. Up to $100,000 of the capital gain recognized because of the deemed disposition could then be sheltered by the exemption. Capital gains that have accrued since that date will be taxable when the property is actually sold or transferred.

Special Cases. *Filing an Election on Eligible Capital Property and Flow-through Entities.* Special rules exist if you filed a February 22, 1994, election on eligible capital property used to carry on a business (usually intangible in the form of goodwill) or on interests in flow-through entities (most commonly, shares of mutual funds or interests in a partnership).

With other capital property, the deemed disposition and reacquisition process immediately increased the tax cost of the property by the capital gains realized at the time of the election. For these two forms of capital property, any gains are recorded in an account called either an "exempt gains balance" (for eligible capital property) or an "exempt capital gains balance" (for flow-through entities). When capital gains are realized on the properties in the future, they can be sheltered up to the amounts in these balances. Separate accounts are created for each specific capital property for which the election was made by the individual.

The exempt capital gains balance account is valid for only a limited amount of time, however. You have until December 31, 2004, to reduce any gains by this account. If the balance is not reduced to zero by that date, the balance amount will automatically be added to the adjusted cost base of the interests still held in the entity. In addition, when you cease to hold an interest in a flow-through entity at any given time, your exempt capital gains balance related to the entity for the taxation years beginning after that date is reduced to zero. In this situation, it is possible to increase the tax cost of the final interests sold, thereby creating a capital loss or a smaller capital gain.

Non-Qualifying Real Property. Real property purchased after March 1, 1992, does not qualify for the capital gains exemption. However, if you owned real property before that date and claimed an exemption on February 22, 1994, any potentially exempt gain will be reduced by the portion of the gain that accrued between March 1, 1992, and February 22, 1994. The increase to tax cost will be equal to the qualifying gain only. It does not affect the value of the property when calculating capital cost allowance (the portion of your capital costs that can be deducted from income on an annual basis).

The $500,000 Exemption

The remaining capital gains exemption may be applied to gains on the disposition of qualified farm property or qualified small business corporation shares. The deduction permitted in computing your taxable income for a year for qualified farm property and qualified small business corporation shares is the least of the three following amounts:

- the unused portion of your maximum capital gains exemption;
- the annual gains limit for the year; or
- the cumulative gains limit at the end of the year.

The unused portion of the maximum capital gains exemption corresponds to the amount of exemption available over your lifetime, less the portion used in previous years (including any portion of the $100,000 personal capital gains exemption used). The annual gains limit for the year equals the amount of the capital gain for the year from the disposition of qualified small business corporation shares or qualified farm property, less deferred capital losses and allowable business investment losses (defined below).

This annual gains limit must be calculated on an annual as well as a cumulative basis. The result is that, for a particular taxation year, the cumulative results of previous years must be taken into account.

Cumulative Net Investment Losses (CNILs). Since 1988, net capital gains eligible for the capital gains exemption have been reduced by all cumulative net investment losses deducted in computing income for taxation years after 1987. Consider your outstanding CNIL as an account that must be reduced before you can claim a capital gains exemption. This reduction prevents you from using your capital gains exemption to offset capital gains and, in the same year, offsetting your other income with investment losses connected with your capital gain. Your CNIL at the end of a year is the amount by which your accumulated investment expenses exceed your accumulated investment income.

Your investment expenses consist of the following items that have been deducted in computing your income for the 1988 and subsequent taxation years:

- Deductions claimed on property that will yield interest, dividends, rent, or other income from property. Such deductions include interest, safe deposit box rental, other carrying charges, and capital cost allowance.
- Carrying charges, including interest, with respect to an interest in, or a contribution to, a limited partnership (unless you are the general partner) or any other partnership where you are not actively engaged in the business of the partnership (unless you carry on a similar business).
- Your share of a loss (except allowable capital losses) of any partnership described above.
- Fifty per cent of your share of deductions attributed to a resource flow-through share or relating to Canadian exploration and other resource expenses of a partnership where you are not actively engaged in the business.
- Any loss for the year from property or from renting or leasing real property owned by you or a partnership, not otherwise included in the investment expenses listed above.
- The amount by which net taxable capital gains realized between March 1, 1992, and February 22, 1994, that are not eligible for the capital gains exemption (e.g., a portion of gains realized on disposition of a vacation or investment property you own in addition to your principal residence) are offset by net capital losses of other years that are deducted by you in the year.

Your investment income for a year essentially consists of the following items that are included in computing income for the year:

- Interest, taxable dividends, rent, and other income from property (including recaptured depreciation in respect of items generating income from property).
- Your share of the income (including recaptured depreciation but not including taxable capital gains) from most limited partnerships or other partnerships where you are not actively

engaged in the business of the partnership (unless you carry on a similar business).

- Income (including recaptured depreciation) for the year from property or from the renting or leasing of real property owned by you or a partnership not otherwise included.
- Fifty per cent of recovered exploration and development expenses included in income.
- The income portion of certain annuity payments, other than those from an income-averaging annuity contract or an annuity purchased pursuant to a deferred profit sharing plan.
- Net taxable capital gains realized on non-qualifying real property (calculated as the gain accruing between March 1, 1992, and February 22, 1994) that are not eligible for the capital gains exemption (e.g., a portion of gains realized on disposition of a vacation or investment property you own in addition to your principal residence).

Whether your capital gains qualify for the capital gains exemption or not, you are still able to deduct the interest paid on funds you borrow for investment purposes. The CNIL rules are concerned only with the calculation of your capital gains exemption.

The interest expense on funds you use to carry on an unincorporated business or profession does not enter into the CNIL calculation.

Your net investment loss is not calculated on an investment-by-investment basis, nor on an annual basis, but rather on a cumulative and pooled basis after 1987 for all of your investment assets. Carrying charges associated with one security may therefore reduce your capital gains exemption available to offset a taxable capital gain realized on the sale of another security. The CNIL rules do not erode your capital gains exemption, but they can delay your use of all or part of it until your cumulative investment income exceeds your cumulative investment expenses.

If you intend to use your exemption in 1998, your CNIL balance at December 31, 1998, will be taken into consideration. If you have a positive CNIL balance, you may wish to take steps to eliminate it.

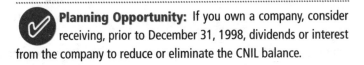

Planning Opportunity: If you own a company, consider receiving, prior to December 31, 1998, dividends or interest from the company to reduce or eliminate the CNIL balance.

Since there are a number of factors to consider, you should consult your professional tax advisor.

Qualified Small Business Corporation Shares. The $500,000 lifetime capital gains exemption can be used to shelter gains arising from the disposition of qualifying shares. The shares must, at the time of disposition, be owned by you (or a person or partnership related to you) and must be shares of the capital stock of a small business corporation.

A "small business corporation" is a Canadian-controlled private corporation (CCPC) of which all or substantially all of the fair market value of the assets is used principally in an active business carried on primarily in Canada (other than a specified investment business and a personal services business). This translates into 90 per cent or more of the fair market value of the assets, according to Revenue Canada. The assets also may be shares in one or more small business corporations connected with the corporation, or a bond, debenture, or similar obligation issued by such a connected corporation.

In addition, the shares must satisfy both a holding period and an active business asset requirement. First, the shares must not have been owned by any person other than yourself or a person or partnership related to you throughout a period of 24 months immediately preceding the disposition. Treasury shares will qualify only if certain conditions are met.

As for the active business asset requirement, more than 50 per cent of the fair market value of the corporation's assets must have been used in an active business throughout the 24-month holding period. This is in addition to the 90 per cent business use requirement applicable at the time of disposition. Assets considered to be used in an active business consist of:

- assets used principally in an active business carried on primarily in Canada by the corporation or a related (associated through common share ownership) corporation; and
- certain shares or debt of connected corporations that are small business corporations.

Qualified Farm Property. The disposition of qualified farm property also entitles an individual to the $500,000 lifetime capital gains exemption (see also Chapter 13 for details on transferring farm property to your child).

> **Caution:** This exemption does not create an additional $500,000 exemption for an individual, but these deductions can be used at the same time, provided that the total capital gain exempted does not exceed $500,000.

To claim the exemption, the qualified farm property must be owned by you, your spouse, or a partnership, if the interest in such partnership is an interest in a family farm partnership of you or your spouse. This last rule enables you or your spouse to qualify for the exemption in situations where the family farm partnership owned the disposed property.

Qualified farm property can be:

- real property (land or building) that has been used in the course of carrying on the business of farming in Canada;
- a share of the capital stock of a family farm corporation of the individual, the individual's spouse, or any of the individual's children;
- an interest in a family farm partnership of the individual, the individual's spouse, or any of the individual's children; and

- eligible capital property (usually intangible, in the form of goodwill or government rights) used in a farming business, to the extent that the disposition of such property creates a capital gain under section 14 of the *Income Tax Act.*

The terms "family farm partnership" and "family farm corporation" both mean an entity that carried on the business of farming in Canada in which the business used more than 50 per cent of the fair market value of all of its property and in which the farmer, the farmer's spouse, or the farmer's child was actively engaged on a regular and continuous basis.

Additional comments are necessary concerning the applicability of the capital gains exemption for the real property mentioned above. The property must have been used in the course of carrying on the business of farming in Canada by:

- the individual;
- a beneficiary of a trust who is related to the person from whom the trust acquired the property;
- the spouse, a child, the mother or father of the individual; or
- a partnership or a family farm corporation in which any one of the above three classes have an interest.

The real property must also meet other requirements to qualify for the exemption. For at least 24 months preceding the disposition, the real property must have been owned by one of the persons mentioned above and:

- for at least two years, the gross revenue from the farming business earned by any one person mentioned above must have exceeded the individual's net income from all other sources; or
- through the 24-month period, the real property must have been used by a partnership or a family farm corporation in the course of carrying on the business of farming in Canada.

In both cases, one of the persons mentioned above must have also been actively engaged on a regular and continuous basis in the farming business.

> **⚠ Caution:** These two requirements restrict the $500,000 exemption only to individuals for whom farming is their main activity.

Relief is provided if the real property was acquired before June 18, 1987, and would otherwise qualify for the exemption if the requirements prior to this date were met, although the current requirements are not. Specifically, the property must have been used for farming in the year of disposition or in at least five years (not necessarily consecutive) during which the property was owned by any person mentioned above.

Non-Exempt Capital Gains and Losses

The following applies to taxpayers who will be taxable on their capital gains or who have incurred capital losses from the disposition of other property.

Rules for Losses. Allowable capital losses, other than "business investment losses" (see below), offset taxable capital gains in the year. Any unused allowable capital losses can be carried back to the three preceding years, or can be carried forward indefinitely to offset taxable capital gains in future years. You may choose the amount of loss carryovers to use and the year in which you use them.

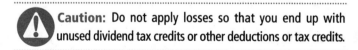

> **⚠ Caution:** Do not apply losses so that you end up with unused dividend tax credits or other deductions or tax credits.

A loss on transfer of property to a corporation controlled by you or your spouse must be deferred until your shares in the corporation are sold.

A loss on transfer of property to your RRSP, your RRIF, or your spouse's RRSP is denied completely.

Planning Opportunity: Consider selling the property to realize the loss, and then transferring or reinvesting the proceeds, taking care to avoid the superficial loss rules (see below).

Settlement Date. Remember that a disposition of shares through a stock exchange is deemed to take place at "settlement date." For Canadian exchanges, settlement date is three business days after the trading date. This means the last trading date in 1998 could be as early as December 24. If the transaction is a cash sale (payment made and share certificates delivered on the trade date), you have until December 31, 1998, to make the trade.

Superficial Loss. You cannot claim a capital loss on an asset that you intend to continue to hold. This rule also applies if the assets are acquired by your spouse, a corporation controlled by you, or any other affiliated person. Where property is sold at a loss and the same asset or "identical" assets are purchased within 30 days before or after the disposition, and the repurchased asset is still held at the end of the thirtieth day following the original disposition, a "superficial loss" results. The person acquiring the replacement asset adds the loss to his or her cost base and the seller of the asset is denied the loss.

 Planning Opportunity: The superficial loss rule does not apply if the assets are acquired by your children or parents.

Identical Properties. Capital properties of a similar kind are subject to special rules covering "identical properties." Stocks of the same class or bonds of identical characteristics of the same corporation are "identical properties." These assets are "pooled," and lose their specific identities.

For example, if 200 shares of a stock are purchased for $8 per share and, subsequently, 100 shares are purchased for $11 per share, the tax cost of the shares is considered to be $9 per share

($2,700 / 300). If the 100 shares purchased for $11 are sold the next day at the same price, you will have a capital gain of $2 per share, and $150 (three-fourths of $200) will be included in your taxable income.

Allowable Business Investment Losses. A business investment loss can occur on the disposition of shares in, or the debt obligations of, a small business corporation (defined in "Qualified Small Business Corporation Shares," above).

 Planning Opportunity: Business investment losses can be used to reduce income from other sources.

To qualify as a business investment loss, the shares or debt must be transferred in an arm's length transaction. This precludes intra-family transfers, but shares of a bankrupt corporation (or one that has ceased operation in limited cases) will qualify. In addition to traditional methods, debt will be considered disposed of if it is established that the debt is uncollectable.

An allowable business investment loss (ABIL) is defined as three-quarters of the total business investment loss. ABILs are treated in the same manner as non-capital losses, such as business losses. You must deduct the allowable portion from all sources of income in the current taxation year first. Any unused losses can be carried back three years and forward seven years.

Caution: Because income in the loss year must be reduced to zero before ABILs can be carried backward or forward, you will be unable to claim your personal tax credits for that year.

You can choose how much of a loss carryover you want to claim in a carryover year. After the seven-year carryforward period, unused ABILs become ordinary capital losses and may be carried forward indefinitely.

To the extent that previous lifetime capital gains exemptions were claimed in previous years, a taxpayer's business investment loss for a taxation year after 1985 is treated as an ordinary capital loss. Similarly, any recognized capital gain is not eligible for the capital gains exemption to the extent of any previous business investment losses realized by the taxpayer after 1984.

Special Cases—Reserves for Proceeds Not Yet Due. If a capital asset is sold, resulting in a capital gain, and the full amount of the proceeds is not due by the end of the year, a part of the capital gain may be deferred by claiming a reserve for the proceeds not yet due. The proceed amounts brought into income each year are treated as ordinary capital gains. These amounts are based on the inclusion rate in the year the reserve is brought into income (not the inclusion rate in the year the asset was sold). Although you may claim less than the maximum available reserve in any year, you cannot claim a larger reserve in the next year.

The *Income Tax Act* requires that the reserve be brought into income and taxed over a maximum period of five years, including the year of disposition.

> **Planning Opportunity:** A ten-year (including the year of disposition) reserve is allowed on the transfer of farm property, shares in a family farm corporation, or shares in a small business corporation to your child, grandchild, or great-grandchild (resident in Canada).

INCOME IN THE FORM OF INTEREST

Debt securities provide income to investors in the form of interest payments. Interest income is added directly to taxable income and taxed at the taxpayer's top marginal rate. Interest is generally taxed in the year you receive it. However, if you buy a debt instrument where the interest is compounded and paid at maturity, you will have to recognize the income annually, or every three years, depending on when you bought the security. Compound interest CSBs and GICs are examples of investments that are subject to the annual or three-year income accrual rules. If your investment qualifies under the three-year accrual rules, you have a ready-made income deferral opportunity

Three-Year Accrual Rules

Only compound interest securities acquired before 1990 are eligible for the three-year accrual rule (e.g., the compound interest version of Canada Savings Bonds Series 44 that was issued in 1989). If an investment held by an individual is subject to the three-year accrual rules, the individual includes in income any interest that has accrued in the previous three years and that has not been previously included.

You may elect in your tax return to include in income any interest accrued (even if not yet paid, as with compound interest) that was not previously included in income, on an annual basis. Once made, the election applies to that particular debt obligation for each subsequent year in which the taxpayer holds the obligation.

> **⚠ Caution:** If you still hold investments that are subject to the three-year accrual rule and the operation of these rules will push your income into a higher tax bracket, reporting annually may be preferable.

Specifically, if you would move from the 17 per cent federal rate to the 26 per cent or 29 per cent federal rate by reporting every three years, consider reporting annually. In making this election, remember that, while you save taxes now, in future years you will end up pre-paying tax.

The interest accrual rules also apply where an individual holds an investment interest in a life insurance policy, including an annuity contract. The rules do not apply to "exempt policies," nor to most investment interests held before December 2,

1982. Certain prescribed annuity contracts are also exempt from the accrual rules.

If a taxpayer acquires a "prescribed debt obligation," interest is deemed to accrue on the obligation. Prescribed debt obligations include zero interest bonds, bonds that are held without also holding the related bond interest coupons, and the interest coupons stripped from such bonds.

Annual Accrual Rules

Individuals who acquired debt investments after 1989 must now report accrued interest on an annual basis.

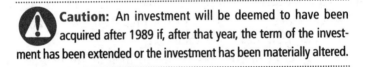

Caution: An investment will be deemed to have been acquired after 1989 if, after that year, the term of the investment has been extended or the investment has been materially altered.

Issuers of most investments subject to the annual accrual rules, including the Bank of Canada, are required to provide annual information slips to the holders of the instruments showing the amount of interest accrued to each anniversary date of the investment.

Planning Around the Accrual Rules

Before investing in deferred income securities or annuities, you should take maximum advantage of deferred income plans for which you are not required to report income on an annual accrual basis: registered retirement savings plans (RRSPs) and registered pension plans (RPPs).

The earnings inside such plans are completely sheltered from tax until you withdraw funds from the plan. RRSP and RPP contributions are generally deductible from income in the current year and payments from a plan can be postponed well into your retirement. Since the deferral is for the long term, you will generally benefit no matter what your marginal tax rate is when you eventually withdraw the funds.

For example, assume that you have the option of contributing $5,000 to an RRSP from which you will begin receiving a retirement income in 20 years. Your marginal tax rate now is 40 per cent, and in the table below it is assumed that your marginal rate in 20 years will be either 30 per cent or 40 per cent. To keep the example simple, it is assumed you will pay tax on the RRSP amount in a lump sum in the twentieth year, which of course would probably not be the case. The RRSP earns interest at the rate of 5 per cent over the 20 years.

Sheltering Effect of RRSPs on $5,000 Invested Now and Held for 20 Years

Future Marginal Tax Rate	After-Tax Amount Available
30%	$9,287
40%	$7,960

If you did not make the RRSP contribution and paid tax at 40 per cent on the $5,000, you would have $3,000 left to invest. Assuming your annual after-tax return is 3 per cent (after paying tax at the rate of 40 per cent on 5 per cent earnings), you will accumulate $5,418 in 20 years, which is $2,542 less than you would accumulate by contributing to the RRSP (40 per cent tax rate after 20 years).

The advantage is that the before-tax amounts in the RRSP accumulate interest on a tax-free basis. Investments made with your after-tax earnings outside an RRSP are taxed each year, leaving you a smaller amount available for reinvestment. In addition, under the RRSP you are able to pay your taxes in the future with inflated dollars that are worth much less than today's dollars.

For a more comprehensive analysis of the retirement saving rules related to RRSPs, see Chapter 14.

> **Planning Opportunity:** Consider the possibility of defer-
> ring tax by acquiring capital property. The accrual rules do
> not apply to unrealized capital gains, and you will not have to recog-
> nize tax until you sell the property.

INCOME FROM DIVIDENDS

Both preferred and common shares can provide income to shareholders in the form of dividends. We limit our discussion to Canadian-source dividend income.

The Taxation of Canadian Dividends

Dividends from Canadian corporations are subject to the dividend tax credit. To calculate the credit, dividends are grossed up by 25 per cent, and the dividend tax credit of 16.67 per cent of the cash amount of dividends received is applied against the total. The following example shows how a top-bracket taxpayer with federal tax payable in excess of $12,500 is taxed on a $1,000 dividend received in 1998.

Taxation of $1,000 Dividend at the Highest Marginal Rate

Cash dividend	$1,000
Gross-up	250
	1,250
Federal tax (29%)	363
Dividend tax credit	(167)
	196
Surtaxes	16
Provincial tax (assume 55%)	108
Total tax	$ 320
Amount retained after tax	$ 680

✓ **Planning Opportunity:** Without argument, you can optimize your tax position using dividends. Depending on the province of residence, an individual with no dependants and with only dividend income could receive approximately $24,000 of dividends in 1998 without paying federal tax.

CREDITS AND DEDUCTIONS RELATED TO INVESTMENTS

Investment Deductions

Fees for investment counselling, portfolio management, and safekeeping are deductible from income earned through your investments. Similar fees charged for self-directed RRSPs are no longer deductible.

Deductible Interest

If you borrow funds to earn income, any interest expense incurred is deductible from income, with certain exceptions. Earning income does not necessarily mean that you have to earn a profit immediately. There need only be a reasonable expectation of profit; therefore, incurring a loss does not prejudice the deductibility of the interest expense. Revenue Canada may disallow the portion of the interest expense that exceeds the return on your investment. This could happen if it was reasonably foreseeable, at the time the loan was taken out, that the rate of interest would exceed the rate of return in the future.

Before 1994, interest expense was deductible only if you continued to own the related investment throughout the period of time the funds were borrowed. Since 1994, you may deduct interest expenses after selling the investment, but only on that portion of the loan represented by the loss realized on the sale of the investment.

You are never allowed to deduct the interest on funds borrowed for personal expenditures, such as interest on money borrowed to finance a vacation or purchase a home.

> **Planning Opportunity:** Borrow only for investment or business purposes and pay for personal expenditures out of your savings. You can deduct interest, however, when a personal asset (such as your home) has been used as collateral for a loan to finance an investment.

Rental Expenses

Although not discussed as a separate category, rent can be viewed either as income from property or as business income. Revenue Canada will accept that you are earning income from property if you rent space and provide basic services only. Basic services include heat, light, parking, and laundry facilities. If you provide additional services to tenants such as cleaning, security, and meals, Revenue Canada is more likely to look on you as operating a business. Generally speaking, the more services you provide, the greater the chance that your rental operation is a business. In that case, you will be required to calculate your income as a business owner (see Chapter 8).

If you earn rental income from an investment property, you may deduct all the current expenses you incur with respect to the rental property and claim capital cost allowance (CCA) on the property itself. CCA applies to depreciable property and allows a deduction of the costs of the property against other income over a period of time.

> **Caution:** CCA cannot be used to create or increase a loss with respect to rental property. It can only offset the net rental income on that, or other, property prior to the CCA claim.

Current expenses include the cost of advertising for tenants, heat, electricity, property taxes, water rates, insurance, and labour and material for routine repairs and maintenance. Capital expenditures such as major additions or renovations are not deductible, but can usually be added to the capital cost of the property and then claimed over time as CCA.

If you rent out part of your principal residence, the same basic rules apply for current expenses and CCA may be claimed for the rented portion. Expenses fully attributable to the rented portion are fully deductible. Common expenses such as heat, electricity, and property taxes must be prorated so that only the portion that relates to the rented part of the principal residence is deducted from rental income. Before you claim any CCA, note that any CCA claimed will erode a proportionate amount of your principal residence exemption. As a result you could be opening yourself to a future taxable gain when you sell your house.

If you are designating your house as a principal residence for years during which you are not occupying it, you cannot claim CCA on it for those years.

If You Invest in Tax Shelters or Offshore

Many upper-income Canadians have discovered the hard way that the quality of a tax shelter investment is by far the most important element. Security for your money should outweigh all other considerations, including immediate tax savings. Receiving a deduction for the money you put into a tax shelter is no consolation if you end up losing your money because the investment is a bad one. If you are considering investing in a tax shelter, read the entire prospectus offering, and obtain professional advice before committing your funds and future state of mind to these high-risk investments.

LIMITED PARTNERSHIPS

The investment tax credits and losses claimed by limited partners are limited to the extent that their investment in the partnership is at risk. Exceptions to these "at-risk rules" are limited to certain partnerships in existence on February 25, 1986, or prospectuses filed before June 12, 1986. The amount at risk for the first purchaser is generally the adjusted cost base (the purchase cost net of expenses incurred in the purchase) of his or her partnership interest at the end of the year plus his or her share of the current year's income of the partnership. This amount is reduced by any amount owing to the partnership and any guarantee or indemnity provided to protect the limited partner against the loss of his or her investment. If allocating losses of a partnership or withdrawing funds results in a negative cost base, the negative amount is considered to be a capital gain of the partner in the year it becomes negative. In spite of the strict rules, limited partnerships frequently offer a good way of arranging financing and limiting risk.

MINERAL EXPLORATION AND OIL AND GAS SHELTERS

With flow-through shares, the various deductions and tax credits associated with oil and gas drilling and mineral exploration flow through directly to the unit holders.

MULTIPLE-UNIT RESIDENTIAL BUILDINGS (MURBs)

Since 1994, MURBs have been treated in the same way as other rental properties owned by persons not actively engaged in the real estate business. Capital cost allowance (CCA) can be used only to reduce rental income to zero, but not to create or increase a loss deductible against other income.

CANADIAN FILMS

In 1987, you could claim your total investment in a certified Canadian film production as capital cost allowance (CCA) over two years. The applicable rate is now 30 per cent per year, calculated on a declining balance basis. A further deduction is granted when annual income from Canadian film productions is sufficient. The change is effective generally for investments acquired after 1987 and before March 1, 1996.

In 1994, new rules were introduced that curtailed perceived abuses relating to these investments. The benefit of CCA on certified Canadian film allocations to produce losses is reduced by any convertible debt that has been put in place to reduce the impact of the "at-risk" rules.

These rules have been replaced by a system of refundable credits to Canadian film producers with no possible flow-out to investors. The new system is applicable to films produced after February 29, 1996.

FARMING AS A TAX SHELTER

Depending on the crop or product raised, and the market for it, farming may be a viable tax shelter. Several rules in the tax law, including a mandatory inventory adjustment, make it more difficult to create losses from farming to offset income from other sources. As well, most taxpayers will be subject to the restricted farm loss rules, which currently limit deductible losses in a year to $8,750.

Farming may be attractive as a tax shelter because of the $500,000 capital gains exemption available for gains on qualifying farm property. Keep in mind, however, that in order to claim the exemption, the farm must be a viable Canadian farming business. If that is the case, you don't necessarily have to be a full-time farmer to take advantage of this exemption.

PROVINCIAL TAX SHELTERS

Many provinces provide incentives to encourage investment in certain areas or industries. For example, some provinces have stock savings plans that provide for tax credits, while others have venture capital plans to encourage investment in small to medium-size companies. Consult with a tax professional in your province to determine which provincial plan suits you.

GENERAL RULES FOR OFFSHORE INVESTMENT REPORTING

Numerous Canadians have offshore investment holdings to reduce exposure of their investment to the unstable Canadian dollar, to take advantage of the rules of lower-tax regimes, or to invest in vehicles that are not available in Canada, among many other reasons. The Canadian government does not discourage its residents from investing offshore, but it does not look kindly upon its residents not paying their full complement of Canadian taxes. The basic rule is that all Canadian residents must declare their worldwide income to Revenue Canada in their annual personal tax return.

Beginning in 1995, Revenue Canada began a massive overhaul of its foreign asset reporting rules. These rules, which require all Canadian resident taxpayers to report specified foreign assets over $100,000, became law on April 25, 1997. The government has delayed implementation of the new rules on several occasions, but has declared that they will be in effect beginning in 1999 for the 1998 tax year. Because this overhaul process is continuing as this book goes to press, this summary of the foreign income reporting requirements is based on the rules as they were known at September 1, 1998. Further, this information is presented only as an overview of the foreign asset reporting requirements. You should consult your tax professional to determine how your investments will be directly affected.

Form T1135

Individuals, corporations, trusts, and partnerships that own specified foreign property with a total cost of more than $100,000 any time during the year must file a T1135 and report those assets. According to Revenue Canada, the categories of foreign property that will trigger the reporting rules are:

- foreign bank accounts, other indebtedness, shares of foreign corporations, real and tangible property, and intangible property situated outside Canada, but not
- property used exclusively for the purpose of carrying on an active business, funds in registered pension plans, personal-use property, and shares in foreign affiliates.

Remember that even if the cost of your foreign assets does not exceed $100,000, you are still required to report any income that you earn on these assets.

Along with the revised reporting rules, there are revised penalties for delayed reporting, under-reporting, and non-reporting of foreign income. Penalties will apply in the case of intentional non-filing for more than 24 months, as well as for under-reporting. The penalty will be calculated on the basis of the cost value of the under- or non-reported assets at the rate of 5 per cent. In the interest of fairness, Revenue Canada will review these penalty provisions after the first two-year review period.

To encourage compliance with the reporting rules, Revenue Canada is introducing the "foreign income verification rule," effective April 30, 1999, for the 1998 tax year. A new form will be introduced in the 1998 tax return that will be in a "check-the-box" format. Taxpayers will not be required to provide a detailed listing of foreign holdings. A taxpayer will check the box that most closely corresponds with the type, location, and range of investment levels, and will also indicate the amount of income from the reported property.

Planning Opportunity: Here are some ways to plan around the reporting rules:

- Your best and easiest method of not reporting is to not hold foreign assets that cost more than $100,000 in total. Dividend reinvestment, for example, will increase the cost base of your foreign investment. Interest payment reinvestment will not.

- Because investment in an active foreign business will not trigger the reporting rules, you might consider this investment option. However, caution must be exercised if you choose this option. The standard for determining whether a business is active is defined by the Canadian *Income Tax Act*. In addition, just as in Canada, investing in an active foreign business carries higher risk than investing in a foreign bank account or mutual fund.

- Invest offshore in assets that qualify as personal-use property. Of course, this option assumes that you maintain an offshore presence. Personal-use property is a broad category and includes capital and non-capital property that is owned for personal use or enjoyment. Under the Canadian rules, the cost base of personal-use capital property is $1,000. If you buy and sell an asset under $1,000, you will not attract any capital gains and need not report any income. Recall also that you can claim a principal residence exemption on a home located outside of Canada. Investing in personal-use property might limit your investment options, but it could be a means of maintaining your cost base of other foreign assets below $100,000 (e.g., diverting your dividends to purchase qualifying personal-use property). In addition, you will not necessarily tie up your foreign investments if you purchase personal-use property that is also a liquid investment.

If You Own Your Own Home

From a tax perspective, the single biggest advantage to owning your own home is that, with a few exceptions, any capital gain that arises on the sale or transfer of your principal residence is exempt from capital gains tax.

PRINCIPAL RESIDENCE EXEMPTION

To qualify for the exemption, you must satisfy the principal residence exemption rules:

1. Only the ownership interest in one home can be designated as your principal residence for a particular year.
2. You can make the designation only for the years you are resident in Canada.
3. For years after 1981, only one principal residence per family unit per year is allowed.

4. The following types of dwellings can qualify as a principal residence:
   - house;
   - condominium;
   - mobile home;
   - trailer;
   - houseboat; or
   - a share in a cooperative housing corporation.
5. The dwelling can be owned outright, or jointly with one or more other individuals.
6. Although your home does not have to be located in Canada to qualify, tax might be payable in the other country upon disposition.
7. For the home to be your principal residence, you, your spouse, or your child must be ordinarily resident in the home during the designated year. Usually the family home is designated, but a part-time residence, such as a summer cottage, can qualify.

> **Caution:** If you have more than one family home and must decide which home to designate and for how many years, the decision can be quite complex and the tax consequences significant. We recommend consulting your professional advisor prior to the sale.

Post-1981 Principal Residence Rules—The Details

Beginning in 1982, a family unit can designate only one home under the principal residence rules with respect to each year. In any particular year, a family unit consists of you, your spouse (provided you had a spouse throughout the year and were not living apart and legally separated), and children who were throughout the year unmarried and under 18 years of age. This means that if you and your spouse each own a home, you will be liable for tax on all or a portion of the capital gain accruing on one of the homes beginning January 1, 1982.

When a couple marries after 1981 and each owns a home, each may designate his or her home for the year of marriage and prior years, but only one home may be designated after the year of marriage. Since 1993, common-law couples have been treated the same as married couples for tax purposes.

Determining the Taxable Portion

The taxable portion of the gain on the sale of a principal residence is calculated by subtracting the exempt portion from the total gain. The remainder, if any, is subject to the normal capital gains rules (see Chapter 9).

The exempt portion is based on the number of years that the property was a principal residence compared to the number of years of ownership. Although the actual rules are complicated, if you can designate the property as your principal residence for all years of ownership, or all years except one, the total gain is generally exempt.

Special transitional rules apply where a property owned on December 31, 1981, is subsequently sold. The rules provide that the non-exempt portion of the gain is the lesser of two amounts. One amount is calculated by viewing the total years of ownership as one period (i.e., the normal method) and the other amount is calculated by separating the years of ownership into two periods, one pre-1982 and one post-1981. To do this latter calculation, the fair market value of the property on December 31, 1981, must be determined.

Designating a Property as a Principal Residence

If, during the year, you dispose of a property that you wish to claim as your principal residence, and you recognize a gain, you have two choices. If a portion of the gain is subject to tax, you must file a prescribed form with your tax return for that year and designate your property as your principal residence for the years chosen. If the gain is completely exempt from tax, Revenue Canada does not require the form to be filed.

Second Homes

If your family currently has, or intends to acquire, a second home, record all capital costs associated with both homes. Capital costs include the costs of adding a pool, finishing the basement, or adding an extra room. These costs will increase the cost base of each home. Unless a record is kept of such expenditures, you may have to compute any ultimate gain using the original purchase price as the cost base, which may be much lower than the total invested in the property.

PLANNING OPPORTUNITIES

The Home Buyers' Plan

The Home Buyers' Plan (HBP) is available only for first-time home buyers who apply after March 1, 1994. "First-time home buyer" means that neither the individual nor the individual's spouse owned a home and lived in it as their principal place of residence in any of the four calendar years beginning before the time of the withdrawal. Individuals may withdraw up to $20,000 from their RRSPs to buy a home without having to pay tax on the withdrawal. A couple can contribute up to $40,000 from two RRSPs. A qualifying home must be acquired before October 1 of the calendar year following the year of the withdrawal, although some exceptions are available.

The withdrawals must be repaid to the home buyer's RRSP in instalments over a maximum period of 15 years. For example, if an individual withdrew $15,000 from an RRSP under the HBP, the scheduled annual repayment would be $1,000 per year ($15,000 divided by 15 years). The 15-year repayment period begins in the next calendar year after the calendar year in which the withdrawal is made. Repayments made in the first 60 days of a year can be treated as having been made in the preceding year (similar to the regular RRSP rules). If, in any year, the individual decides not to repay the scheduled amount, or decides to repay only part of it, the amount that is not repaid will be included in the individual's income for the year and, consequently, will be subject to tax.

> **⚠ Caution:** In addition to your normal RRSP contributions every year, you should restore the funds taken from your RRSP as quickly as possible to maximize your retirement income.

You are allowed to repay more than the scheduled annual repayment in any year. This results in a lower outstanding balance and lower scheduled annual repayments for the remainder of the pay-back period.

A special rule denies a tax deduction for contributions to an RRSP that are withdrawn within 90 days under the HBP. Contributions within the 90-day period are not considered to be withdrawn except to the extent that the RRSP balance after the withdrawals is less than the amount of the contributions.

> **NEW** **New for 1999!** The federal government has proposed in its 1998 budget to introduce legislation that will permit individuals to participate in the HBP more than once under certain circumstances.
>
> The federal budget has also proposed legislation that will permit a disabled person, or a supporting individual, to withdraw funds from an RRSP under the HBP even if they currently own a home. To qualify, the funds must be used to purchase a home that is more accessible or better suited to the individual's personal needs. The disabled individual must qualify for the disability tax credit to be eligible.
>
> These new rules only apply to RRSP funds withdrawn after 1998.

Home Office Expenses

Certain home office expenses can be deductible, provided that the office is your principal place of business, or is used exclusively to earn business income and is used on a regular and continuous basis for meeting clients, customers, or patients. The amount deducted cannot exceed the income from the business for the year, after other expenses are deducted. Any excess amount may be carried forward to be deducted in years when the business generates income.

Income Splitting

If the family has only one house, consider selling ownership of the personal residence to the lower-income spouse at fair market value. This will ensure that any potential taxable gains that may arise when the house is sold will be taxed in the tax bracket of the lower-income spouse. A taxable gain could arise if the house is used for something other than a principal residence (i.e., to earn rental or business income). Note that to ensure Revenue Canada will not attribute the taxable gain to the high-income spouse, the high-income spouse must elect in his/her tax return that the sale take place at fair market value and the low-income spouse must actually pay fair value consideration.

To Sell or Not to Sell

Consider retaining your residence if you are leaving it on an indefinite or temporary basis. During your absence, you may rent your home and still retain your ability to designate it as your principal residence for the years in which you were living in it and, provided certain conditions are met, for up to four years after that.

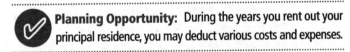

Planning Opportunity: During the years you rent out your principal residence, you may deduct various costs and expenses.

If you sell the residence instead of reoccupying it, the gain that accrued during the years in which you designate the home as a principal residence will be tax-free. The gain that accrued during the years when the residence was rented may not be taxable if it was rented for less than five years.

Special rules will extend the four-year maximum period if you have moved because your employer or your spouse's employer required that you or your spouse relocate. Certain conditions must be met to take advantage of this extension.

If You Have a Spouse

DEFINITION OF SPOUSE

Several years ago, Revenue Canada expanded the definition of spouse to include common-law spouses. Same-sex couples are not considered married for the purposes of the *Income Tax Act*.

CREDITS AND DEDUCTIONS

Spouse Credit

In 1998, a person who at any time in the year is a married individual (including common-law) supporting a spouse with net income of $538 or less may claim a federal married tax credit of $915. The credit is reduced by 17 per cent of the spouse's net income in excess of $538. No credit is available for a spouse whose net income is $5,918 or more.

If you live apart from your spouse at the end of the year by reason of marriage breakdown, any reduction in the spouse credit is calculated using your spouse's income for the year while married and not separated.

You may claim the credit for only one person. If you divorce and remarry in the same year, you cannot double the credit. The federal spouse tax credit is indexed annually according to increases in the Consumer Price Index above 3 per cent.

Pooling of Credits

Planning Opportunity: A simple method of income splitting involves the splitting of family expenses. The higher-income spouse should pay all the expenses and taxes for the family, while the lower-income spouse invests all available savings. Income from the investments will be taxed in the hands of the lower-income spouse at a lower rate while the higher-income spouse can claim all available credits.

The following can be transferred between spouses:

• Medical expenses (see Chapter 6);
• Mental or physical impairment credit (see Chapter 13);
• Tuition fee credit (see Chapter 13);
• Age 65 and over credit (see Chapter 16);
• Pension income credit (see Chapter 16);
• Charitable donation credit (see Chapter 18).

PLANNING OPPORTUNITIES

Income Splitting

There will be overlap between the income splitting strategies we discuss in this chapter and those we cover in Chapter 13. More detailed descriptions of the strategies appear in this chapter. Remember that successful income splitting requires that you and your spouse (or children, as the case may be) are taxed in different tax brackets. Shifting income between two individuals in the same tax bracket will not achieve any tax savings. In addition, the more complex the plan, the more important it is that you consult your tax planning advisor to ensure that the attribution rules will not reverse any tax savings. The attribution rules are the biggest barrier between you and successful income splitting with your spouse.

Business Income. If your spouse earns income from funds that you have loaned or transferred to him or her, the attribution rules generally apply to attribute the income back to you. To get around these rules, your spouse must personally run the business or invest in a partnership in which he or she actively participates. Further, the attribution rules also should not apply if you and your spouse operate a business as a bona fide partnership. Capital gains that arise on disposition of the business by your spouse will be attributed to you, however.

The *Income Tax Act* makes a distinction between the loaning of money and the loaning of property. If you have loaned or transferred property that is an interest in a partnership to your spouse (or your child), your spouse's share of the business income of the partnership may be considered income from property and not income from business. As a result, the attribution rules may apply, and the partnership income may be attributed back to you. This provision will apply where your spouse is a "specified member" of the partnership. According to the *Income Tax Act*, a specified member is someone who:

- was a limited partner of the partnership during the fiscal period in which the income arose, and
- was neither actively engaged in the activities of the partnership nor carried on a business similar to that of the partnership (other than as a member of the partnership) on a regular, continuous, and substantial basis throughout the period.

For example, if you give or lend your spouse $100,000 that is used to acquire an interest in a limited partnership, the attribution rules may apply because your spouse is only a passive investor. If your spouse's share of the partnership income is $10,000 for a given year, that $10,000 will be added to your income for the year.

Interest on Interest. The attribution rules do not mean that you should abandon the idea of giving or loaning your spouse funds to earn investment income. Interest on interest is generally not subject to the attribution rules and amounts earned this way can be significant in the long run. For example, assume that you give your spouse $20,000 and it is invested to earn 8 per cent annually over the next 10 years with the interest paid annually and reinvested at this same rate. Over the 10 years, only the simple interest of $16,000 (8 per cent of $20,000 = $1,600 × 10 years) will be attributed to you. Interest on interest of $7,178, over and above the simple interest of $16,000, will be earned over the 10-year period, if the annual interest of $1,600 is reinvested at 8 per cent, and it will be taxed in your spouse's hands, not in yours.

There is no attribution of income earned on attributed income, such as interest on interest, unless the attributed income is a stock dividend.

> **Planning Opportunity:** Although the income or gain is attributed for tax purposes, these amounts still legally belong to your spouse. For this reason, this type of income is considered almost creditor-proof, meaning that your creditors are largely unable to access these funds.

Spousal Registered Retirement Savings Plans. Details on spousal RRSPs are contained in Chapter 14.

Overall, spousal RRSPs are an effective method of achieving future income splitting because the attribution rules will not apply when your spouse begins withdrawing from the plan. The annuity or registered retirement income fund (RRIF) payments that will provide retirement income for your spouse are taxable only in the hands of your spouse.

If you foresee the need to withdraw RRSP funds in the near future, you should stop contributing to a spousal RRSP for at least two years. Any funds withdrawn from your spouse's RRSP can be attributed to you if you contributed to any spousal RRSP during the year or during the two years preceding the withdrawal.

Remember that amounts contributed to a spousal RRSP belong to your spouse. Because of this, a spousal RRSP is another way of creditor-proofing your money to some degree. If you contribute to your spouse's RRSP, make the payment directly to the trustee and have a receipt created in your name, so that you can prove you made the payment.

Pay Your Spouse's Taxes. This amount is considered a gift by you to your spouse. Of course, no income would be earned on the amount since it is used to pay taxes and therefore there would be no attribution. Your spouse could then invest the funds that otherwise would have gone to pay his or her taxes, and any income earned on these funds would not be attributed back to you. This arrangement does not apply where your spouse's taxes are deducted at source by an employer.

Who Pays the Family Expenses? If both spouses are earning income but one spouse will continually have a higher tax rate than the other, the higher-income spouse could pay all or most of the family expenses while the lower-income spouse invests all or most of his or her earnings.

The income generated from these investments will be taxed at a lower rate and is not attributable.

Pay Your Spouse a Salary. You may pay your spouse a salary for work performed in your unincorporated business, and deduct the salary in determining your income from the business. The amount will be taxed in your spouse's hands. The salary or wages paid must be reasonable in relation to the duties performed. Your spouse can then contribute to the Canada Pension Plan and will also have earned income and can contribute to an RRSP.

> **Planning Opportunity:** If you are operating a sideline business that has a reasonable expectation of medium-term profit, and you pay your spouse a reasonable salary, you could create a loss in the business for a given year. This may be useful if you can apply the loss to other sources of income.

Spousal Business Partnerships. Even though you may pay a salary to your spouse, in some cases you may want to characterize the business as a partnership. As a partner, your spouse is entitled to a share of partnership profits as well as a proportionate share of the liabilities. This situation is common in farm operations, but can also apply to any type of business.

⚠️ **Caution:** Have a properly documented partnership agreement detailing the profit-sharing arrangements and ownership of assets of the business.

If Revenue Canada considers the allocation of the partnership income to be unreasonable, it will change it to an allocation that it considers reasonable in the circumstances.

If the spouse's capital contribution to the business is significant, a spousal partnership will be more advantageous than paying the spouse a salary. This could permit a larger share of the business profits to be recognized by the spouse than if the spouse were paid a reasonable salary for duties performed.

✅ **Planning Opportunity:** If you cannot establish a spousal partnership, consider incorporating the business. Your spouse could participate by owning shares acquired with his or her own funds.

Transfers at Fair Market Value. You can elect to transfer property to your spouse and receive fair market value consideration for it. The attribution rules will not apply (if certain conditions are satisfied), and future income and capital gains will be taxed in your spouse's hands. For capital property, you must recognize any accrued capital gains or losses at the time of the transfer.

If property with unrealized capital losses is transferred at fair market value, the superficial loss rules (see Chapter 9) come into play, and you will be denied the capital loss if the property is still owned by your spouse 31 days after the transfer.

Gift Interest Expenses to Your Spouse. Because the attribution rules apply only where there is income or a capital gain earned on transferred funds, give your spouse funds to pay the interest on a loan made by you to your spouse to earn income. No attribution will arise on the amount gifted for the interest expense, nor on the net income earned by the spouse from the loaned funds.

The loan must be a bona fide loan, interest must be charged at the lesser of the prescribed rate for tax purposes and commercial rates, and the interest must be paid within 30 days of the year-end.

You must include the interest paid by the spouse in your income for tax purposes, but you will benefit because the spouse's investment income will compound much more quickly since it is not being diluted annually by an interest payment on the loan.

Using Transferred Funds for Leverage. Attribution will not arise on income or capital gains earned on funds borrowed commercially by your spouse, provided there is no guarantee by you. As a result, if you are considering borrowing for investment purposes, transfer funds to your spouse to enable him or her to borrow. For example, you might give your spouse $25,000 in order for him or her to borrow $75,000. The spouse then buys $100,000 worth of securities, which would be lodged as collateral with the lending institution in lieu of your guarantee. In this situation, only 25 per cent of any net income or capital gains earned ($25,000/$100,000) would be attributed to you.

Locking in the Best Rate on Spousal Loans. If you intend to lend funds to your spouse, charge interest at the rate prescribed by Revenue Canada. This rate likely will be lower than commercial lending rates. The prescribed rate is set each quarter based on 90-day Treasury Bill yields of the first month of the preceding quarter. This allows the rate for any quarter to be known two months in advance. Before locking in the interest rate on a spousal loan for any longer than three months, check the direction the prescribed rate will move in the next quarter. If the rate is expected to increase, and you do not expect rates to fall again, consider setting the term of the loan for an extended period. If the rate is expected to decline, keep the loan on a variable-rate basis.

Professional Management Companies. Professional management companies are popular because the attribution rules do not apply to small business corporations. Such companies are generally set up by professionals such as doctors or dentists who are not allowed by their governing bodies to incorporate. The company, which is owned by the spouse and/or children of the professional, provides services to the professional and charges a fee, usually 15 per cent above the cost of the services. Such services could include the rental of equipment and facilities, the services of assistants, and bookkeeping, secretarial, and administrative services. Professional advice should be sought to ensure the company will not be considered a personal services business. The *Income Tax Act* applies limitations on expenses and affects the rate of tax a personal services business will pay.

If it is incorporated, a professional management company is considered a small business corporation and no attribution of income will occur if the professional lends or sells assets to a small business corporation and your spouse or children are shareholders. If the management business is unincorporated, which is generally not advisable, and assets are transferred to the spouse and used to earn business income, there would be no attribution of that income.

Depending on the nature of services provided, fees billed for these services may be subject to the GST/HST and, in Quebec, the Quebec Sales Tax. Some activities, such as most health care services, do not qualify for a reimbursement of the GST/HST and QST paid. In such cases, a professional management company provides no advantage.

Situations to Avoid—Application of the Attribution Rules

Caution: Some of the following suggestions are "aggressive," i.e., the tax authorities may not take kindly to taxpayers using them. If you are considering any of these aggressive techniques, consult your professional advisors to identify any possible disadvantages. In many cases, you will not be worse off if the plan is scuttled, since the attributed income or capital gain would have been realized in your hands in any case.

No Attribution Occurs. There are very clearly defined guidelines that determine when the attribution rules will cease or not apply at all. Any event outside these guidelines will trigger the rules.

If you have transferred income or property to a related minor, attribution of income ceases the year the child turns 18 (for exception, see "Property Loans to a Non-Arm's Length Party" below). In the case of a spouse, attribution ceases upon divorce or when the spouses are living separate and apart by reason of marriage breakdown. The transferor/lender spouse must file an election (which is a joint election with the transferee/borrower spouse) to prevent the attribution of capital gains after the breakdown of a marriage. Attribution also stops when a lender or transferor dies or ceases to be resident in Canada.

Income from certain loans or transfers is not subject to attribution if:

- interest is charged on the loan at a reasonable rate or at the rate prescribed for income tax purposes at the time the loan was made, and
- the interest payable for each year is paid within 30 days after the end of that year.

In the case of a transfer, there is no attribution if:

- the fair market value (FMV) of the transferred property does not exceed the FMV of the consideration received by the transferor on the transfer;
- in the case where the consideration received includes debt, the conditions listed above for an exempt loan are met; and
- in a transfer to a spouse, the transferor elects not to have the tax-deferred rollover provisions apply.

The following are situations where the attribution rules always apply and, consequently, where tax savings are nearly impossible to achieve. We discuss the rules in relation to spouses and children.

Transfers to Your Spouse or Minor Child. The attribution rules apply if an individual lends or transfers property to, or for the benefit of, a spouse (or future spouse) or certain minors, or a trust established for such a person. The attribution rules apply to minors (under age 18) with whom the individual does not deal at arm's length (child, grandchild, brother, sister, brother-in-law, sister-in-law, etc.) and to an individual's niece or nephew.

Rules similar to the attribution rules apply where property is lent to any non-arm's length person, such as an adult child. Property includes money, shares, bonds, a right of any kind, a home, land, etc. The word "transfer" has been interpreted very broadly and can include a gift or a sale at fair market value.

If the attribution rules apply, income (or losses) from lent or transferred property, or from property substituted for it, is not taxed in the hands of the recipient, but is included in the income of the individual who made the loan or transfer. In most cases, it is the net income or loss from the property that is attributed to the lender or transferor.

The attribution rules also apply to capital gains and losses realized by a spouse on lent or transferred property or substituted property. There is no attribution of capital gains or losses realized by a minor (under age 18 throughout the taxation year), except in certain cases involving farm property that has been previously given preferential tax treatment.

Capital gains are only attributable to the transferor for transfers occurring after 1971. Thus, a capital gain arising from property transferred before 1972 is not attributable, but any income earned on that property, such as dividends, is attributable to the transferor.

> ⚠️ **Caution:** Attributed income retains its character (except in corporate attribution situations). If you lend funds to your spouse, who then invests the funds in preferred shares, any dividends, capital gains, or capital losses on the preferred shares will be attributed back to you. You will then be taxed on the attributed amounts as dividends, capital gains, or capital losses.

Attribution Rules and Trusts. For there to be attribution of income (or loss), the spouse or minor child must have an income (except in certain corporate situations). Consequently, if property is transferred to a trust for the benefit of minor children and the income from the property is taxed in the trust, there is no attribution of income. All of the income of an *inter vivos* trust (a trust created during your lifetime) is taxed at the highest personal tax rate and no advantage would be gained, however.

If the income is paid or payable to the children from the trust, it constitutes income and the attribution rules will apply. On the other hand, a net loss suffered by a trust cannot be allocated to beneficiaries, with the result that there can never be attribution of trust losses.

If the attributed income is earned through a trust, special rules apply to determine the amount of trust income of a designated beneficiary (i.e., the spouse, minor child, minor niece or nephew) that will be attributed. These rules will produce different results depending on whether all or only a portion of the income earned by the trust is from "lent or transferred property," or whether there is more than one designated beneficiary.

> **Caution:** If you and your spouse each decide to contribute funds to the same trust, which includes your minor child as a beneficiary, the income of that minor could be attributed to both you and your spouse, leading to double taxation.

To avoid this, each parent should create a separate trust. The income of only one trust would then be attributed back to the parent who created it.

If you are involved in trusts, review your situation and ensure that you do not inadvertently stumble into unfortunate tax complications.

Substituted Property. The attribution rules apply not only to lent or transferred property but also to property that is substituted for the lent or transferred property. If you lend funds to your spouse, who then uses the funds to acquire preferred shares, the shares are considered substituted property and the attribution rules will apply to the income from, and the capital gains or losses on, the shares. If the preferred shares were sold and the funds were used to acquire bonds, the bonds would be substituted property to which the attribution rules would apply.

Substituted property encompasses stock dividends received on a share. They will be considered property substituted for that share. The attribution rules will apply to any income earned (and in the case of a spouse, any gains realized) on a stock dividend that was received as income on lent, transferred, or substituted property.

Property Loans to a Non-Arm's Length Party. The attribution rules apply if you lend property to any individual with whom you do not deal at arm's length. If it is reasonable to consider that one of the main reasons for the loan is to reduce or avoid your tax liability on income from the property (or property substituted for it), the loan will trigger the attribution rules.

A non-arm's length party is an individual who is related to you by blood (both forebears and descendants), marriage, or adoption. Parents, spouses, and even adult children are affected. The outright transfer of property (e.g., by gift) to a non-arm's length individual does not create adverse tax consequences.

The typical situation covered by the non-arm's length rule is a low-interest or no-interest loan made to your adult child. Commercial rate loans are exempted. If, however, the rate of interest is less than both the prescribed interest rate for income tax purposes (announced quarterly) and the rate that arm's length parties would have agreed to under similar circumstances when the loan was made, income attribution will apply. It will also apply if the interest on the loan is not paid within 30 days after the end of each year. If the debtor spends the funds for a non-investment purpose (e.g., paying tuition fees), there is no income to attribute.

Corporate Attribution Rules. These rules, in effect since October 27, 1986, apply to loans (including transfers) between individuals that are routed through certain corporations. There will be deemed attribution of interest income to the transferor if it can be determined that one of the main purposes of the loan is to reduce the transferor's income and to benefit a "designated person." If the transferor receives (as a minimum) an annual prescribed return on the debt or shares in return for the loan or transfer of property, there will be no attribution. A designated person is a spouse or certain minors if they own at least 10 per cent of any class of shares of the corporation.

The corporate attribution rules do not apply to small business corporations (SBCs) that qualify as Canadian-controlled private corporations (CCPCs) that carry on an active business in Canada. Both public corporations and CCPCs that hold portfolio investments or real estate are excluded from this exception.

Potential problems for intra-corporate loans include:

- Attribution can occur if the shareholders of the corporation that receives the loan include the individual's spouse, certain minors, or a partnership or trust in which the spouse or a minor is, respectively, a member or a beneficiary.
- Unlike the normal attribution rules, the spouse or a minor need not receive income for the corporate attribution rules to apply.

Corporate attribution rules do not apply when the shares of the corporation are held in trust, and under the terms of the trust the individual may not receive any of the capital or income of the trust while he or she is a designated person (spouse, related minor, niece, or nephew).

CONSEQUENCES OF MARRIAGE BREAKDOWN

Marriage breakdown, or the dissolution of a common-law union, create numerous legal consequences, but our discussion is limited to the tax issues. The following tax principles or strategies will be affected by marriage breakdown. Because this is not an exhaustive list, ensure that your professional advisors are aware of your situation.

• The good news is that the attribution rules no longer apply.
• Opportunities exist for settlements to be transferred to your ex-spouse's tax-deferred investment vehicle.

You will no longer be able to claim a deduction for contributing to a spousal RRSP; however, the money already deposited will continue to be your spouse's property. The rules discouraging the collapsing of spousal RRSPs do not apply on the breakdown of a marriage.

On the breakdown of a marriage, funds may be transferred from one spouse's RRSP or RRIF to the other spouse's RRSP, RRIF, or RPP on a tax-deferred basis. The attribution rules are not triggered by such an RRSP transfer. In order not to be taxed, payments made from your RRSP to your ex-spouse's RRSP must be pursuant to a decree, order, or judgment of a competent tribunal or a written separation agreement.

• There are tax issues related to alimony and maintenance payments.

If you are divorced or separated, you may be receiving (or paying) amounts of alimony and/or maintenance. These payments are included in your income in the year of receipt (and are deductible for the payer in the same year). These payments are very different from child support payments, which are no longer included in the income of the recipient or deductible from the income of the payer. The general rule is that if a payment is taxable income to one party, it is an allowable deduction to the other and vice versa.

Alimony or maintenance must be:
– periodic;
– pursuant to a decree, judgment, or written agreement, and
– made for the maintenance of the recipient and/or children.

In addition, the parties to the agreement must be living apart pursuant to a divorce, judicial separation, or written separation agreement, from the time of the payment until the end of the year. The issues are further complicated by additional considerations: whether the payments are periodic alimony or maintenance versus instalments of lump-sum obligations, and whether payments made to third parties qualify as alimony or maintenance. A third-party payment includes home mortgage payments or rental payments to a landlord. If a payer is making both alimony as well as child support payments, unless a third-party payment is clearly defined as part of the spousal support payments, it will be considered child support under the new rules. Voluntary additional payments that are not part of the agreement will not qualify as either alimony or maintenance.

⚠️ **Caution:** Ensure that you receive competent legal and tax advice regarding payment arrangements under separation and/or divorce agreements. The new Federal Child Support Guidelines came into effect May 1, 1997.

Frequently, alimony and maintenance agreements result in income shifting from a higher-income individual to a lower-income individual. As a result, there are tax benefits inherent in the payments because the higher-income individual obtains a deduction that saves a greater amount of tax than the corresponding tax cost to the recipient of the payment. Because of the shifting aspects of these payments, many separation or divorce agreements are negotiated on an after-tax basis.

• There are also tax consequences related to child support payments.

Child support paid pursuant to a written agreement or court order made on or after May 1, 1997, will neither be deductible by the payer, nor be included in the income of the recipient for tax purposes. Existing child support orders will remain unaffected unless varied after April 30, 1997, to change the amount of the child support.

After May 1, 1997, where the payer and the recipient of child support agree and file a joint election with Revenue Canada, they will be able to move to the new rules for payments after May 1, 1997, even if their agreement is not varied. Agreements entered into or court orders after March 5, 1996, can provide that the new rules will apply for payments made after May 1, 1997.

These tax changes do not apply to spousal support. Periodic payments of spousal support pursuant to a written agreement or order will be tax-deductible to the payer and taxable to the recipient.

⚠️ **Caution:** If an agreement or order does not clearly distinguish the amount of spousal support from child support, the entire amount will be deemed to be child support.

For this reason, expenses paid to third parties will be treated as child support unless they are clearly identified in the agreement or order as being solely for the benefit of the recipient spouse. As well, child support will be deemed to have been paid before spousal support in cases of partial payment of the agreed amount.

CHAPTER THIRTEEN

If You Have Children

IF YOU HAVE CHILDREN OR GRANDCHILDREN UNDER 18: CREDITS AND DEDUCTIONS

Equivalent-to-Spouse

If you do not claim the spousal amount (see Chapter 12) and you support a related person, you may be able to claim an "equivalent-to-spouse" credit of $915 in 1998. To qualify for the credit, you must be unmarried or living apart from your spouse and neither supporting nor being supported by your spouse. The credit is reduced if the dependant's income exceeds $538 and is indexed annually according to increases in the Consumer Price Index above 3 per cent.

Child Tax Benefit and the Working Income Supplement

These two credits were in place until July 19, 1998. The child tax benefit (CTB) was a non-taxable benefit paid monthly to families, usually to the mother. The annual benefit of $1,020 per child increased by $75 for the third and each subsequent child. An additional $213 per child under age seven was available; however, this component of the benefit was reduced by 25 per cent of child care expenses claimed.

For low-income families, the child tax benefit also included a working income supplement (WIS), calculated on a per-child basis. The maximum level for a one-child family was $605, $1,010 for a two-child family, and an additional $330 for the third and each subsequent child.

The WIS benefit was reduced for families earning more than $20,921, and the total CTB was reduced for families earning over $25,921. The CTB and WIS were not subject to income tax, and were indexed annually according to changes in the Consumer Price Index above 3 per cent.

Canada Child Tax Benefit

New for 1998! Effective July 1998, the child tax benefit and the working income supplement were replaced by the Canada child tax benefit (CCTB). The benefits payable under the CCTB are essentially the same as under the previous programs. If you previously received the CTB and the WIS, you automatically begin receiving the CCTB.

Revenue Canada also administers provincial and territorial child benefit and credit programs for Quebec, British Columbia, Alberta, Saskatchewan, New Brunswick, Nova Scotia, and the Northwest Territories. Revenue Canada will automatically use the information provided for the CCTB to determine your eligibility for these programs.

Child Care Expenses

New for 1998! To further assist low-income families, the child care expense deduction was increased to a maximum of $4,000 per child between the ages of 7 and 16 at any time during the year, effective January 1, 1998. The maximum deduction per child is increased to $7,000 for claims in respect of severely disabled children and children under seven years of age at the end of the year.

For federal tax purposes, the deduction is restricted to two-thirds of earned income and must be claimed by the lower-income spouse. In Quebec it is a refundable tax credit, which either spouse can claim. Generally, this credit is limited to the full earned income of the lower-income spouse.

PLANNING OPPORTUNITIES

Income Splitting

Subject to the attribution rules (discussed in Chapters 3 and 12), there are opportunities to split your income with your minor children. For details on these arrangements, refer to Chapter 12; in particular, review the section on "Situations to Avoid—Application of the Attribution Rules."

The following income splitting strategies can be applied specifically to your children.

Transferring the Canada Child Tax Benefit

This is the most common method of generating income that is taxable in the hands of a child. Revenue Canada, administratively, considers the income earned under the CCTB to be earned by the child for which it is paid, even though the cheque is issued in the name of a parent. Therefore, the funds may be invested in the child's own investment vehicle, such as a savings account, mutual fund, bond, or investment certificate, and the income earned on these funds will not be attributed back to the parent. Benefits received under the provincial child benefit programs generally do not qualify for this planning opportunity.

Transferring Capital Property

Although income earned on property transferred to your child will be attributed back to you, capital gains will not. This fact opens up many possibilities for transferring property, particularly property that will not qualify for the $500,000 capital gains exemption. Non-qualifying property includes shares of public or private corporations and units in growth equity mutual funds that provide capital gains income. Ensure that any arrangements you make comply with the attribution rules (see Chapter 12).

Exception: Farm Property Transfers to a Child

During your lifetime, you can transfer farm property to a child, grandchild, or great-grandchild. You may choose the value for the transfer of the property at any amount between your adjusted cost base (the cost of the property plus the costs incurred to purchase it) of the farming property and its fair market value. The child assumes a tax cost equal to the transfer value and becomes liable for any tax on capital gains on disposition.

⚠️ **Caution:** If the child sells the farm property, including farming assets, before the year he or she turns 18, and the property was transferred to the child at less than fair market value, any resulting capital gain will be attributed to you.

To be a qualifying farm property, the assets must be used principally in the business of farming. The transferor, the transferor's spouse, or any of the taxpayer's children must actively farm the property on a regular and continuous basis immediately before the transfer, and the child must be a Canadian resident. Such a tax-deferred transfer is also allowed for an interest in a qualifying farm partnership and shares of farm corporations.

A full $500,000 capital gains exemption is available to you on the disposition of qualified farm property (see Chapter 9). If you have already claimed the full exemption under the $100,000 lifetime exemption (available until February 22, 1994), the remaining available exemption totals $400,000.

Unless you expect to fully use your exemption in the future, your children will benefit (i.e., will have a smaller gain to realize in the future) if you transfer the farm property at a value above your cost and recognize all or a portion of any resulting gain that would be exempt under your $500,000 lifetime capital gains exemption.

Testamentary Planning for Your Grandchildren

Because estate planning is an ongoing process, you should continually update your will and adapt it to your most current situation. If your children are now grown and have their own minor children, consider bequeathing funds in your will in trust to your grandchildren rather than to your adult children. On your death, the funds will go in trust, with your children as trustees, to the minor grandchildren. There is no attribution because the attribution rules cease to apply on your death. Your grandchildren can earn income on the bequeathed funds and be taxed at a much lower rate than if their parents (your children) had earned the income. As trustees, the parents could direct the trust to use the funds and income for the benefit of your grandchildren (e.g., education costs).

IF YOUR CHILDREN ATTEND POST-SECONDARY SCHOOL AND/OR ARE OVER 18: CREDITS AND DEDUCTIONS

Tuition Fees

The 1998 federal tuition fee tax credit is 17 per cent of eligible tuition fees paid in respect of a calendar year. Tuition must be paid to a qualified institution for courses at the post-secondary school level, or to an institution certified by the Minister of Employment and Immigration (for courses intended to provide occupational skills to a student who is at least age 16 at the end of the year). An occupational skills course must demand a fee of at least $100. Special rules extend the tax credit to eligible tuition fees paid by a full-time student enrolled at a university outside Canada. The credit also covers fees in excess of $100 paid by a Canadian resident who commutes to an educational institution providing courses at the post-secondary level in the United States.

Only tuition fees paid for programs held during the tax year are eligible to determine the tuition tax credit for that year. If tuition fees cover the costs for an academic session extending beyond the year, the portion covering the excess period is eligible in determining the tuition tax credit for the next year. For example, if the session covered by the tuition fees extends from September of one year to April of the next year, the tuition tax credit is computed for each of those years as one-half of the total tuition fees paid multiplied by 17 per cent.

Eligible tuition fees include mandatory ancillary fees imposed by universities. Fees levied by student bodies for non-educational purposes are not included in eligible tuition fees.

Education Amount

NEW **New for 1998!** The federal education tax credit for 1998 is $34 ($200 x 17 per cent) for each month in the year during which the student was a full-time student in a qualifying program at a designated educational institution. The tax credit for a part-time student is $10.20 ($60 x 17 per cent). To claim the tax credit, the student must file a certificate issued by the educational institution.

Unused Tuition and Education Amounts

Students who cannot fully use the tuition or education amount credit to reduce taxes payable may now carry forward any unused tuition fee credit or education tax credit to a later year.

Alternatively, the student may transfer any unused portion (up to $850) of the tuition fee tax credit and the education tax credit to his or her spouse. If the spouse did not claim the student as a dependant and did not claim any of the student's unused tax credits that could have been transferred to the spouse, the student's supporting parent or grandparent can claim the student's unused tuition fee and education tax credits (to a maximum of $850). A prescribed form, available from the institution, must be filed by the parent or grandparent making the claim

NEW **New for 1998!**

- In addition to being able to claim the education credit, part-time students are now eligible to deduct child care expenses related to their course time.
- Because many students now leave a post-secondary program with $25,000 in student loan debt, the federal government is providing a tax credit to individuals while they pay down their loans. The credit is 17 per cent of interest on eligible student loans. Eligible loans include those that are issued under the Canada Student Loans Act or an equivalent provincial statute. Note that interest on student loans obtained outside of the government student loan program, such as those offered by most major banks, generally will not qualify for this tax credit.

PLANNING OPPORTUNITIES

Maintaining a Dependant's Status

If your child has generated RRSP contribution room by earning qualifying "earned income," you may want to contribute to an RRSP on behalf of the child. Your child will be able to lower his or her taxable income by claiming the contribution on his or her next tax return. If the child's taxable income is lowered sufficiently, you can then claim a portion of the child's tuition fee and education tax credits, if applicable.

RRSP Withdrawals

NEW **New for 1998!** An individual may now withdraw funds from his or her RRSP to fund attendance at an eligible post-secondary institution. A maximum of $10,000 may be withdrawn in any year, with a maximum withdrawal of $20,000 over a four-year period. The amount withdrawn must be repaid after graduation in minimum equal payments over a 10-year period. Any amounts not repaid in a particular year must be included in taxable income.

Registered Education Savings Plans (RESPs)

Although a parent who contributes to an RESP will not receive a tax deduction for the contributions, there is a long-term tax advantage to these plans. Contributions will grow tax-free until your child becomes entitled to the savings or the plan is otherwise dismantled. When your child receives the income, it will be taxed in his or her hands, and will not be attributed back to you. In this way, RESPs provide another opportunity for some degree of income splitting.

The annual limit for contributions is $4,000 per child to a maximum of $42,000 per child. If your child does not attend post-secondary school, up to $40,000 of RESP income can be transferred on a tax-deferred basis to your own RRSP. Any excess income withdrawn from an RESP is subject to a tax of 20 per cent in addition to any normal taxes payable. To take advantage of the $40,000 transfer limit:

- you must have sufficient contribution room available in your RRSP;
- the RESP must have been in existence for at least 10 years; and
- your child must be at least 21.

RESPs can now also be used to fund the cost of distance education, provided it is equivalent to a full-time course load.

Canada Education Savings Grant (CESG)

NEW **New for 1998!** Contributions to an RESP made after January 1, 1998, are now eligible for a CESG of 20 per cent for the first $2,000 contributed. Catch-up contributions in excess of the $2,000 limit made in later years will also qualify for the CESG.

IF YOUR CHILD HAS SPECIAL NEEDS: CREDITS AND DEDUCTIONS

Dependent by Infirmity

If a person is dependent on you by reason of mental or physical infirmity and is 18 years of age or older at any time in the year, you may claim a dependant tax credit of $400 in 1998. The credit is eroded if the dependant's income exceeds $4,103, and is reduced to nil if the dependant's income is $6,456 or more. The credit is indexed annually according to increases in the Consumer Price Index above 3 per cent. Revenue Canada requires that a doctor provide a statement supporting the infirmity before allowing a taxpayer to claim this credit.

The equivalent-to-spouse credit can also be claimed for children with special needs. However, you must choose between claiming either the dependant credit or the equivalent-to-spouse credit for any one dependant. You may claim both credits if you have two dependants that qualify for the respective tax credits.

If more than one individual is entitled to claim a dependant tax credit for the same dependant, the total claimed by the individuals must not exceed the maximum allowed if only one individual had made the claim. Revenue Canada is permitted to allocate the total tax credit to the supporting individuals if they cannot agree on an allocation.

Mental or Physical Impairment

A person with a severe and prolonged mental or physical impairment that has been certified by a medical doctor or optometrist may claim a federal tax credit in 1998 of $720. This federal credit is indexed annually according to increases in the Consumer Price Index above 3 per cent.

Any unused portion of the credit may, under certain circumstances, be transferred to a spouse or to another person who supported the individual.

If You Have an RRSP

The registered retirement savings plan (RRSP) program is the best tax deferral opportunity for average Canadians. An RRSP will allow you to invest pre-tax employment or self-employment or any other form of "earned" income within specific limits, and any income earned in the RRSP is not taxed until withdrawn. Eventually, the accumulated amount in your plan is paid back to you as retirement income from your RRSP or a post-RRSP plan, such as a registered retirement income fund (RRIF). Tax is payable only when you withdraw funds or begin to receive a retirement income from the RRSP.

RRSPs may also be used effectively for saving for a down payment on a home, going back to school full-time, or taking a year's sabbatical from your job. Withdrawing RRSP funds for these purposes should be done only as a last resort. Withdrawing money defeats the main RRSP function of generating an adequate retirement income.

MAKING AN RRSP WORK FOR YOU

Because your RRSP contribution allows you to claim a deduction on your income tax return, you save the tax that you otherwise would have had to pay on the amount of the contribution. The saving gives you more money to invest within the RRSP than you would have if you paid the tax and used after-tax dollars to invest outside an RRSP. As the time value of money principle demonstrates, if you pay the tax now, those dollars are gone forever. If you contribute to an RRSP, you can use those tax dollars as part of your investment program and, depending on your age, you may enjoy the tax deferral for a very long time. Optimizing the time value of your money now can give you a powerful boost toward a financially worry-free retirement.

The longer the funds remain in your RRSP, the greater their growth when compared with funds invested outside the RRSP. That's why you should begin making RRSP contributions as early in your working life as possible.

> **Planning Opportunity:** The earlier you begin contributing to an RRSP, the more you contribute each year, and the earlier you contribute each year, the more funds you will have available in the RRSP for retirement income.

If you fail to contribute or to maximize your contributions as early as possible, the amount of RRSP money available to provide your retirement income will be reduced. Your future retirement income will be smaller as a result.

In addition, the higher the earnings rate for your investments, the faster they will grow within an RRSP as compared to growth outside. Your RRSP contribution gives you a larger sum to invest than you would have if you paid tax and invested only after-tax dollars.

CONTRIBUTION RULES AND RRSP MECHANICS

Contributions can be made each year and are deductible from income for tax purposes, within specific limits, in the year they are made or a subsequent year.

Planning Opportunity: Contributions made in the first 60 days of the year are deductible in that year or in the immediately preceding year. Starting in 1991, unused deduction room for a given year, up to the allowable contribution limit, may be carried forward for use in subsequent years.

Any income or capital gain arising in the RRSP is not immediately subject to tax, provided certain requirements are met.

Caution: Capital gains and dividends lose their special tax status when earned within an RRSP and are fully taxed when withdrawn.

Although you must weigh this special tax status against the value of long-term tax deferral in your RRSP, capital gains and dividends may best be earned outside the RRSP. You will be able to use the dividend tax credit, the preferential income inclusion rate for capital gains, or the $500,000 lifetime capital gains exemption. If these credits are not available or are of limited value to you for your dividend or capital gain income, the RRSP remains an effective tax deferral mechanism (refer to "Plan Your Investments: Interest, Dividends, or Capital Gains in Your RRSP" below for further considerations).

Who Can Contribute?

Canadian residents and in certain circumstances non-residents with earned income (defined below) can contribute to an RRSP. Since you must arrange to receive a retirement income from your RRSP by December 31 of the year you turn age 69, no further contributions to your own RRSP can be made past this date. If you are 69 or older, you can still contribute to a spousal RRSP if your spouse is under age 69. If you have not yet reached age 69, but you are receiving an RRSP retirement income, you may continue to contribute to your own RRSP, provided that you still have earned income.

Children under the age of 18 may contribute to an RRSP, assuming they have "earned income" and meet RRSP contribution rules. However, you may have trouble finding an issuer willing to enter into an RRSP contract with a minor. Some taxpayers have made contributions (for which no deduction is received) to their child's RRSP to split income with the child and reduce the family's overall tax bill. Depending on how long the funds are left in the RRSP and the child's tax rate at the time the funds are withdrawn, the tax deferral advantage may be sufficient to offset your increased tax cost. To avoid penalty taxes, the child must have deductible RRSP room. Moreover, there is no reduction of the penalty taxes for the $2,000 "excess contribution" limit unless the RRSP owner attained age 18 in a prior year.

Contribution Limits
For Individuals Who Are Not Members of RPPs or DPSPs.
The RRSP contribution limit for individuals who are not members of registered pension plans (RPPs) or deferred profit sharing plans (DPSPs) is 18 per cent of the prior year's earned income to a specific dollar maximum. Note that some participants in special plans, such as certain foreign retirement plans, may be treated as if they were participating in an RPP. For the years 1996 to 2002 inclusive, this maximum amount is set at $13,500.

For example, the maximum RRSP contribution for 1999 is 18 per cent of earned income in 1998 to a maximum of $13,500. To put it another way, if you want to contribute the maximum of $13,500 to your RRSP in respect of 1999, you need earned income in 1998 of at least $75,000.

For Members of DPSPs or Money Purchase RPPs. For members of DPSPs or money purchase RPPs (accumulated contributions and earnings in the plan are used at retirement to purchase the best possible pension), the RRSP contribution limit is 18 per cent of the previous year's earned income to the dollar maximum for the current year, minus the "pension adjustment" (PA). The PA for these individuals is simply the total of all employee and employer contributions and reallocated forfeitures made in the previous calendar year to all money purchase RPPs and DPSPs.

For example, assume that in 1998 your employer contributes $1,800 to your money purchase RPP and you contribute $1,600 to the plan. Your earned income in 1998 is $50,000, which means that your maximum RRSP contribution for 1999 is $9,000 (the lesser of $13,500 and 18 per cent of $50,000). From this you must deduct your PA from the previous year (1998) of $3,400 (RPP contributions of $1,800 and $1,600). Thus, your allowable RRSP contribution in 1999 is $5,600 ($9,000 minus $3,400).

For Members of Defined Benefit RPPs. For these individuals (who are guaranteed a specific pension through their RPP), the RRSP contribution limit is 18 per cent of the previous year's earned income to the dollar maximum for the current year, as noted above, minus a PA that reflects the value of accrued benefits under the RPP in respect of the previous year and any past service pension adjustment (an amount that reflects retroactive enhancements to the plan) reported in the year, and increased by any pension adjustment reversals reported in the year. The pension adjustment reversal is reported where an individual ceases to participate in a registered plan and the amount received from the plan (other than retirement income or a deferred annuity) is less than the pension adjustments reported while the taxpayer participated in the plan. Pension adjustment reversals will be most common when a taxpayer leaves a defined benefit RPP, but also may arise when a member ceases to participate in a DPSP or money purchase RPP. If the individual is also a member of a DPSP or money purchase RPP, the PA will reflect the amount of any contributions and forfeitures under these plans.

Pension Adjustment for a Year

The PA is designed to ensure that RPP (or DPSP) members in different plans, with similar incomes but different benefit rates, have equal access to tax assistance to help build their retirement income. The PA for a calendar year is used to determine the RRSP deduction limit for the following year.

For example, a member of a pension plan that provides generous benefits will have a relatively high PA. A high PA will lessen the individual's ability to contribute to an RRSP. Many members of non-contributory defined benefit plans have found that they cannot contribute to an RRSP. Less generous pension plans will result in a smaller PA and larger allowable RRSP contributions.

Employers must calculate PAs for each employee and report them on the T4 required by the last day of February each year. Once employees receive their T4 and consider the past service pension adjustments and pension adjustment reversals reported in the year, they can determine precisely their RRSP contribution limit for the following year. Revenue Canada also advises taxpayers of their RRSP deduction limit on their income tax assessment for the preceding year.

Earned Income Defined

Your RRSP contribution limit is based on a percentage of your earned income. Earned income for a Canadian resident includes:

- salary or wages minus any allowable deductions from this income (other than RPP contributions, contributions to a retirement compensation arrangement (RCA), and deductions for a clergyman's residence);
- disability pensions paid under the Canada Pension Plan or Quebec Pension Plan, provided you were resident in Canada when you received the payments;

- income from royalties in respect of a work or invention of which the taxpayer was the author or inventor;
- income from carrying on a business, either alone or as a partner actively engaged in the business;
- net rental income, whether active or passive, from real property;
- payments from supplementary unemployment benefit plans;
- alimony or maintenance included in income for tax purposes (including that received by a common-law spouse), as well as reimbursements received by you of alimony or maintenance payments you paid;
- net research grants;

less the following:

- losses from carrying on business either alone or as a partner actively engaged in the business;
- net rental losses from real property;
- deductible alimony or maintenance payments, as well as reimbursements paid by you of alimony or maintenance payments you received;
- certain negative cumulative eligible capital amounts that have been included in business income.

Non-residents use different rules to calculate earned income.

Carry Forward Rule

If you contribute less than the maximum allowable amount to your RRSP in any particular year, the "unused RRSP deduction room" can be carried forward. This means that you can make contributions of more than the maximums otherwise permitted in later years.

> ⚠️ **Caution:** Waiting until later years to make up deduction room carried forward may result in a tax cost and in many cases will result in a smaller accumulation in the RRSP by the time you retire.

There also appears to be little point in delaying your contribution to a later year when you expect your tax rate will be higher. Your tax saving may be offset by the cost of giving up the tax shelter advantage that you could have gained from earlier contributions. However, in some situations, it may be worthwhile to defer claiming the deduction. For example, if your earned income were to increase significantly for one year, you would benefit from being able to claim a larger RRSP contribution deduction for that year.

Withdrawals from an RRSP—Including the Educational Leave Option

RRSPs are intended to be held until retirement, at which point you establish a retirement income program. There are no government restrictions against withdrawing funds from most RRSPs at any time, however. The amount withdrawn is included in income for tax purposes, although if the withdrawal relates to a non-deductible excess RRSP contribution, an offsetting deduction may be available.

You may withdraw funds tax-free to be used for a down payment on a principal residence under the Home Buyers' Plan (see Chapter 11).

NEW **New for 1999!** The Home Buyers' Plan requirements are being loosened for disabled individuals. These measures take effect in 1999. You may be able to participate in the plan even if you do not qualify as a first-time home buyer. Under the general rules, a first-time home buyer is an individual who has never previously owned a home, as well as an individual who has not owned a home since before January 1, 1994. Note that if you have resided with a spouse in a home owned by the spouse in the periods discussed above, you will not qualify as a first-time home buyer.

NEW **New for 1998!** You are now able to make tax-free withdrawals from your RRSP to cover the costs of going back to school full-time in a qualifying program. Programs that require full-time attendance for periods of three months or longer will qualify. You are entitled to withdraw up to $10,000 per year to a maximum of $20,000 over four years. In general, the pay-back provisions require that you pay back the withdrawals in equal instalments over 10 years, beginning no later than 60 days after the fifth year following the year of the first withdrawal.

Caution: As with the Home Buyers' Plan, before you make your withdrawal, consider the immediate cash benefit over the long-term effects on your retirement savings. Consider also how you will be able to pay back the withdrawals as well as continue to make contributions to your plan.

Apart from these tax-free withdrawal programs, you may withdraw any amount from your RRSP for your own reasons, if your plan allows it. Some plans require you to provide up to one or two months' notice for withdrawal. Pre-1986 RRSPs must be amended by the issuer to allow a partial withdrawal. The issuer of the RRSP is required to withhold tax at the following rates on any RRSP amount paid to you:

Withholding Tax Rates for RRSP Withdrawals

| | Canadian Residents | |
Amount	Outside Quebec (%)	Inside Quebec (%)
$5,000 or less	10	25
$5,001 to $15,000	20	33
Over $15,000	30	38

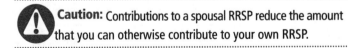

Planning Opportunity: If you are withdrawing relatively large amounts from an RRSP or a RRIF, make several separate withdrawals to lessen the withholding rate, and perhaps make withdrawals over several years to avoid a significant increase in your marginal tax rate.

Spousal RRSPs

Any amount of your regular allowable RRSP contribution can be contributed to a spousal RRSP, whether or not your spouse makes his or her own RRSP contributions. You are entitled to claim an RRSP contribution deduction for the amounts contributed to your plan and to the spousal plan. Under a spousal RRSP, your spouse is the only annuitant.

Make the contribution directly to the trustee of the plan and have a receipt made out in your name so that you can prove that you made the payment.

Spousal RRSP contributions are extremely valuable for splitting retirement income. For example, assume your spouse has few or no other sources of pension income, apart from those from the government. If your spouse's marginal tax rate will be 25 per cent on retirement while yours will be 45 per cent, you and your spouse will have up to an extra 20 cents on every dollar of RRSP retirement income available if you contributed to a spousal plan. Expressed in percentage terms, your after-tax disposable income on the RRSP amounts after retiring could increase by over 36 per cent. In addition, your spouse will have income eligible for the tax credit on pension income when he or she reaches age 65.

Caution: Contributions to a spousal RRSP reduce the amount that you can otherwise contribute to your own RRSP.

In other words, the total of amounts contributed by you to both plans is limited by your total deduction room available. You may not transfer amounts from your own RRSPs or RPPs to a spousal RRSP, except on marriage breakdown or death.

If you are 69 years of age or older and have deduction room available, you may still make contributions to your spouse's RRSP if he or she has not reached age 69.

Within 60 days of the end of the year in which a taxpayer dies, it is possible for the legal representative of an estate to make a contribution to a spousal RRSP if the spouse is under age 69. This creates a deduction equivalent to the contribution on the deceased's final return of income.

Withdrawals from a Spousal RRSP. If your spouse receives funds from any of his or her RRSPs after you have made a spousal contribution, from any commuted annuity from a spousal plan, or from any registered retirement income fund (RRIF) that received funds from a spousal plan in excess of the minimum amount required to be paid from the RRIF, you could be taxed on the withdrawn amounts. The taxable amount will be equal to the lesser of:

(a) the amount received by your spouse, or
(b) the aggregate of your contributions to any spousal plans that were made in the same year your spouse receives the funds and the two preceding calendar years (excluding amounts already added back to your income for those two years).

The excess, if any, of (a) over (b) is included in your spouse's income. For example, assume you contribute the following amounts to a spousal RRSP:

	Amounts Contributed	
Year	By You	By Spouse
1	$2,000	—
2	—	$4,000
3	$1,000	—

If your spouse removes $4,000 from the RRSP at the end of Year 3, $3,000 is included in your income and $1,000 is included in your spouse's income. If your spouse contributed the $4,000 to a separate, non-spousal plan in Year 2 and then withdrew the $4,000 in Year 3, the entire amount would be included in your spouse's income, assuming you had not made a contribution to that particular plan.

This restriction on withdrawal applies regardless of the number of different RRSPs your spouse may have or whether funds have been transferred from a "spousal" RRSP to another RRSP to which no spousal contributions were made directly. If your spouse receives funds from his or her own RRSP, the amounts are not included in your income, even though you may have made spousal RRSP contributions to other plans within the prescribed period.

The withdrawal restriction does not apply on your death, or if you are divorced or separated and living apart from your spouse.

Locked-In RRSPs

Upon termination of employment, employees can do one of the following: leave their pension entitlements with their former employer; transfer them to a pension plan with their new employer, if the new employer agrees; or transfer them to an RRSP.

The RRSPs usually employed in this situation are locked-in plans, which are more restrictive than ordinary RRSPs. They do not provide for withdrawals prior to retirement. In addition, the typical locked-in RRSP will provide that, upon your retirement, you must purchase an annuity, or a life income fund, using the plan funds. Certain provincial pension laws already require this treatment on transfers from RPPs to RRSPs.

Types of Contributions

You can contribute either cash or property to an RRSP depending on the type of RRSP you have. Managed RRSPs generally allow only cash contributions, whereas self-directed RRSPs allow a much broader variety of contributions. Nevertheless, the value of your contribution of property is the fair market value of the property at the time of contribution. For tax purposes, a deemed disposition will occur upon the transfer to the plan, resulting in a capital gain or loss. Any gain must be included in income for tax purposes.

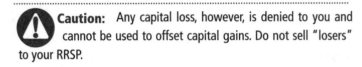

Caution: Any capital loss, however, is denied to you and cannot be used to offset capital gains. Do not sell "losers" to your RRSP.

If you contribute a non-qualified investment (defined below), the fair market value of that investment is included in computing your income for the year of contribution.

Should You Borrow for Your RRSP Contribution?

Because any interest paid on funds borrowed to make an RRSP contribution is not deductible for tax purposes, try to limit your investment borrowing for non-RRSP investments. But it is better to borrow to make a contribution than to not contribute at all. Make a contribution now rather than waiting several years to begin sheltering income from tax in the RRSP. Before you borrow, try to ensure that your earnings inside your RRSP are growing at a higher rate than your interest payments.

Transfers to and from an RRSP

Tax-free transfers between plans, up to a prescribed maximum, are possible if the transfers are made directly and in lump sums. For example, tax-free transfers can be made directly from one RRSP to another RRSP, RRIF, or RPP. RRSP amounts can only be transferred by the issuer of the RRSP and must be done before the maturity of the plan. If you receive the amount directly, it will be included in your taxable income.

Planning Opportunity: The tax-free rollover of a retiring allowance into an RRSP is still allowed, subject to certain limits.

A retiring allowance is a payment made in recognition of long years of services and paid as compensation for a loss of office or employment, including retirement. For the years of employment before 1996, the limit is $2,000 per year of service. Up to and including 1988, this may be increased by $1,500 for each year for which no employer contributions to an RPP or DPSP are vested. The employer should make the transfer directly to the RRSP to avoid withholding taxes.

Planning Opportunity: Provided that the general transfer conditions are satisfied, a retiring allowance can be an effective mechanism for a self-employed individual or small business owner to enhance his or her RRSP holdings. The key is to ensure that the amount received as a retiring allowance will qualify as reasonable in the eyes of Revenue Canada. If the payment can be characterized as a deferral of compensation, the tax-free transfer will not be allowed.

Annuity and RRIF payments are also transferable between RRSPs or other RRIFs. You are allowed to make direct transfers of commuted annuity amounts and payments from a RRIF in excess of the required minimum payment (see below) to an RRSP or another RRIF. You can also use these transferred funds to acquire any of the RRSP-type annuities. The purchased annuity must provide for equal annual or more frequent payments, starting not later than one year after the transfer.

A payment received by you as a spouse or dependent person (if no spouse) from the RRSP of a deceased person can also be transferred tax-free to your RRSP. Finally, a tax-free transfer of RRSP amounts to your spouse on marriage breakdown is also possible.

Penalties, Special Taxes, and Deregistration

Excess Contributions. When undeducted RRSP contributions exceed a certain limit at the end of a month, a 1 per cent penalty tax is imposed on the amount in excess of $2,000 until this amount is withdrawn. Transition rules are provided for taxpayers with overcontributions on February 26, 1995, that do not exceed an $8,000 limit. These overcontributions can be retained in the RRSP without penalty and deducted as contributions for 1996 and subsequent years, until the limit is brought down to $2,000.

> ⚠ **Caution:** You cannot claim a deduction for any new contributions until you have written down your overcontribution.

> **Planning Opportunity:** Consider maxing out your overcontribution allowance in the year you turn 69 to maximize your RRSP holdings.

Foreign Investments. As the wavering world value of our Canadian dollar occasionally reminds us, there are more stable currencies available in the global markets. For this reason, just as foreign investments will provide a stabilizing effect for your non-RRSP investments, so too will they benefit your RRSP investments. Generally, you are allowed to invest 20 per cent of the cost of your RRSP investments in qualified foreign securities. If you exceed this level, your RRSP is subject to tax at the rate of 1 per cent per month on the excess amount invested in foreign securities for each month the excess remains in the RRSP.

> **Planning Opportunity:** You can exceed the 20 per cent limit, within certain limits, if you make investments in eligible small businesses or invest through certain trusts. In addition, you can also maximize your foreign holdings by investing in mutual funds that have a high percentage of foreign investments. Consult your tax advisor.

Non-Qualified Investments. If your RRSP acquires an investment that is not a qualified RRSP investment, the fair market value of the investment at the time of acquisition is included in your income in that year. In the year the RRSP disposes of the investment, you may deduct from your income the proceeds of disposition or the amount previously added to income, whichever is less.

 Caution: Tax is payable at the top marginal rate by the RRSP on the income earned by the non-qualified investment.

If a qualified investment in your RRSP becomes a non-qualified investment, the RRSP must pay a special tax equal to 1 per cent of the fair market value of the investment at the time of acquisition for each month the investment retains its non-qualified status, or until the investment is disposed of by the RRSP, assuming the value of the investment was not included in your income.

Borrowing Money or Carrying on Business. If your RRSP borrows money at any point in the year, tax is payable by the RRSP on all its income each year until the borrowed funds are repaid. An RRSP is a trust and is subject to tax at the maximum personal rate in your province of residence.

If the RRSP carries on a business at any time during the year, the resulting business income is subject to tax at regular trust rates.

RRSP as Collateral for a Loan. If any of your RRSP property is used as collateral for a loan, the fair market value of the property used as collateral is added to your income in that particular year. When the RRSP property ceases to be used as collateral, an amount equal to the amount previously added to income less any losses suffered on the loan transaction may be deducted from income. If the RRSP is a deposit plan, it will be subject to deregistration should any of the RRSP be pledged, assigned, etc. In that case, the entire amount in the plan is included in your income for tax purposes and there is no way that the plan can be subsequently reinstated.

Deregistration. RRSPs can be deregistered for a variety of reasons. The fair market value of all of the assets of the particular plan are included in your income for tax purposes in the year the plan is deregistered. Rest assured that most issuers structure an RRSP to prevent it from being deregistered in most circumstances (i.e., the contract or arrangement you have with the issuer will prohibit actions that would result in deregistration).

An RRSP will automatically be deregistered if you do not arrange a retirement income to be paid by December 31 of the year you turn age 69. The plan is effectively deregistered on the first day of the following year and its full value is included in income in the year you turn age 70. Some plans provide for an automatic annuity purchase if no other retirement income is arranged, but an annuity may not suit your retirement income needs.

RRSP INVESTMENTS

Plan Your Investments: Interest, Dividends, or Capital Gains in Your RRSP

If all your investments are held inside an RRSP, your investment strategy should be to maximize your return over the long term. Remember that all amounts received from RRSPs are included in your taxable income and taxed at your marginal rate. As a result, capital gains and dividends earned in an RRSP lose their identity and are not eligible for preferential tax treatment.

If you have investments both inside and outside RRSPs, the rules of thumb are somewhat different. First, interest-bearing investments should be held in the RRSP because interest income is taxed at full rates outside your RRSP. Second, dividend-paying preferred shares or common shares generally should be held inside an RRSP if you anticipate realizing significant non-exempt capital gains on these investments in future. If the choice comes down to holding either equities or interest-earning investments in your RRSP, you should opt to retain the interest-earning investment within the plan. Capital investments that qualify for the $500,000 lifetime capital gains exemption should be held outside the plan to take full advantage of that benefit.

Your age also plays a factor in choosing the most appropriate investments for your RRSP. Generally, the younger you are, the more heavily you can weight your portfolio in favour of equities. Since you are investing for the long term, you can take advantage of the expected higher return over this period. You will be able to weather the ups and downs of the stock market. The closer you are to retirement, however, the more heavily your RRSP (and non-RRSP investments) should be weighted toward less risky investments such as interest-bearing securities to protect your accumulated capital.

Canada Deposit Insurance

Determine if your RRSP investments are covered by the Canada Deposit Insurance Corporation (CDIC), or other comparable deposit insurance programs. The other insurance plans are established on a provincial basis for deposits made with credit unions and caisses populaires. CDIC-covered investments include savings and chequing accounts, and guaranteed investment certificates and term deposits that are redeemable within five years. The insurance does not apply to foreign currency deposits (such as U.S. dollar savings accounts or U.S. dollar GICs) or mutual funds.

The maximum insurance coverage provided by CDIC is $60,000 per customer per member institution. The coverage available to members of credit unions and caisse populaires varies by province and is at least equal to the CDIC coverage.

Planning Opportunity: If you have RRSPs with more than one member institution, whether directly or through a self-directed plan, your coverage is multiplied.

Similarly, if you have a self-directed RRSP that holds investments from various member financial institutions, each of these investments will be covered separately. CDIC insurance on your RRSP is separate from CDIC insurance on investments you hold personally, which in effect doubles your maximum coverage at one institution to $120,000.

Types of RRSPs

There are three major categories of RRSP investment vehicles:

- insurance-type, where you contract to pay a certain amount, usually periodically, in return for a retirement income of a certain size, also paid periodically;
- deposit RRSPs, where your deposits are made directly with the issuer; and
- RRSP trusts, of which the most common are self-directed RRSPs where you make the investment decisions.

Within these types of RRSPs, there are two further categories: managed and self-directed. Managed RRSPs are, as the name implies, managed for you by the insurance company, mutual fund company, bank, or other financial institution. A financial institution will also hold your self-directed RRSP assets, but you are able to make your own investment decisions.

Overall, insurance companies sell RRSPs that are similar to and competitive with RRSPs sold by other financial institutions. Life insurance RRSPs usually are not protected under the CDIC, although they are self-insured by the insurance industry.

Self-Directed RRSPs

Self-directed RRSPs enable you to choose from the full complement of allowable RRSP investments. Managed accounts offer more limited choices. According to Revenue Canada, qualifying RRSP investments include:

- money, but not foreign currency or gold;

- bonds and debentures of the Government of Canada, a province, municipality, or Crown corporation, including Canada Savings Bonds and stripped bonds;
- Canadian guaranteed investment certificates (GICs);
- shares and debt obligations of Canadian public corporations listed on a Canadian exchange;
- shares listed on a specified stock exchange outside Canada;
- shares of the capital stock of certain public corporations not listed on a Canadian exchange;
- units of a mutual fund trust;
- a mortgage secured by real property inside Canada, including a mortgage on your own house (provided certain market rate interest rules are satisfied);
- real property, if it is acquired as a result of a default under a mortgage investment held by the RRSP
- an annuity, provided that payments do not commence until the RRSP matures;
- a warrant or future listed on a Canadian exchange; and
- certain limited partnership interests.

Self-directed RRSPs generally provide convenient monthly reporting from one source and can help you diversify to reduce risk. As investment objectives change over time, the make-up of a self-directed investment portfolio can be updated, providing maximum flexibility.

SPECIAL SITUATIONS

RRSPs and Non-Residents

The tax consequences of becoming a non-resident can be extremely complex. Deciding how to deal with your RRSP should be considered in conjunction with the many other financial and tax decisions you must make at that time, and should be made with professional guidance. In very general terms, tax is withheld from many types of payments originating in Canada and made to residents of another country. The other country also may tax the "payment," but most give credit for any Canadian taxes already paid. The Canadian tax treatment of RRSP amounts generally depends on whether the RRSP has matured, and also on your new country of residence.

> **Planning Opportunity:** If your departure from Canada is not permanent, you need not dismantle your RRSP; you can let it continue to grow on a tax-deferred basis for Canadian tax purposes.

If you are working abroad, however, your foreign income may not qualify as earned income and you may not be able to continue to make contributions to your plan.

Creditor Access to Your RRSP

The courts have decided that creditors can gain access to a bankrupt's RRSP to settle debts. Only some insurance-type RRSPs offer any creditor protection, although recent case law may have created a chink in that armour. Creditors cannot gain access to life annuity payments, and they may have trouble seizing term-certain annuity payments or the funds in a RRIF. Switching your RRSP to an insurance company shortly before you declare bankruptcy probably will not offer any protection, because the bankruptcy laws "see through" these types of transactions.

RRSPs on Death

The tax treatment of RRSP amounts on the death of the annuitant depends on whether the RRSP has matured and on the identity of the beneficiary.

> **Planning Opportunity:** To ensure that RRSP amounts go to the intended beneficiaries with as little trouble as possible, name specific RRSP beneficiaries in the RRSP contract or in your will.

If the RRSP has not matured, generally the fair market value of all RRSP property is included in the taxable income of the deceased in the year of death as determined in the final income tax return. As a result, tax may be payable before the funds can be distributed to the beneficiaries.

There are two exceptions. First, if a spouse (including a common-law spouse) is named as beneficiary, the plan can be transferred to the spouse on a tax-deferred basis. Second, a "refund of premiums" is not included in the deceased's income.

A refund of premiums, which generally includes accumulated income, is defined as either:

- any amount paid to the deceased annuitant's spouse from the RRSP, even if the spouse was not specifically named as a beneficiary, or
- if the annuitant had no spouse at the time of death, amounts paid to dependent children or grandchildren who were financially dependent on the annuitant.

A spouse, or a physically or mentally infirm child, may transfer a refund of premiums to his or her own RRSP or RRIF on a tax-deferred basis in the year of the annuitant's death or within 60 days after the end of that year. In addition, a spouse or a mentally or physically infirm child may purchase a life annuity or term-certain annuity to age 90 with the refund of premiums. Other children who receive a refund of premiums may set up an annuity that runs until they reach 18 years of age.

The legal representative (executor) of the deceased's estate may elect for either the spouse or, if there is no spouse, qualifying dependants to receive a refund of premiums.

Somewhat similar rules apply to RRIFs. If the deceased's spouse is the beneficiary, the plan is essentially transferred to the spouse on a tax-deferred basis, and the spouse receives all future payments.

MATURING YOUR RRSP

The decisions to be made before your RRSP matures are not automatic. Careful consideration must be given to your retirement goals, the amount of money that will be required to achieve those goals, and the time at which the money will be required. The tax impact of arranging for your retirement income should also be examined. It is necessary to weigh RRSP retirement income options carefully. Competent professional advice is recommended to assist you in planning for your retirement income.

Maturity Options

RRSPs must be matured before December 31 of the year in which the annuitant turns age 69.

"Maturing" an RRSP simply means making arrangements for receiving a retirement income from accumulated RRSP funds. In the case of some insurance RRSPs, it is the date you begin receiving the stipulated RRSP income. With non-insurance RRSPs, there are three main maturity options. First, you can arrange to receive an annuity, of which there are several types. Second, you can transfer the accumulated RRSP funds into a RRIF from which a periodic retirement income is received. Third, you can collapse the RRSP and receive a lump sum after paying the relevant tax.

You can choose any or all of the options and have as many different types of annuities and RRIFs as you want. This flexibility allows you to arrange the type of retirement income you need to suit your expected income requirements. For example, you might consider collapsing a portion of your accumulated RRSPs to finance spending in the early years of your retirement (e.g., for extended travel), although this can also be accomplished with a RRIF. You also probably want to build in a certain amount of inflation protection by transferring some of your RRSP funds to a RRIF and/or indexed annuity.

Even after choosing your retirement income options, your plan can remain flexible. You can switch from option to option with relative freedom. For example, you can switch a RRIF to another issuer to earn a better return. As well, you can have as many RRIFs as you like. You can also withdraw any amount from any RRIF at any time, although a minimum amount must be withdrawn from each RRIF each year. You also may be able to commute RRSP annuities, depending on the terms of the contract, in which case the commuted amount becomes taxable.

Amounts withdrawn from a RRIF in excess of the required minimum amount and commuted annuity amounts may be directly transferred on a tax-deferred basis to other annuities or a RRIF, or even to an RRSP if you are under age 70. You also may be able to buy an impaired health life annuity from some life insurance companies, which provides for larger payments if you can establish that your life expectancy is considerably shorter than normal.

 Planning Opportunity: You do not have to acquire an annuity or RRIF from the issuer of your RRSP.

Shop around for the best rates on the options you want, and consider using an annuities broker or other professional advisor to search for the best rates and make arrangements for you.

Caution: Do not miss the legislated deadline (the year in which you turn age 69); otherwise, all accumulated funds in your RRSP will be included in your taxable income in the year following the year you turn 69. You will have no recourse for correcting this oversight.

Consequence of Early Maturity

Maturing your RRSPs early can be expensive in terms of reduced income. Try to delay maturing your RRSPs until you absolutely must, or mature only a portion of your accumulated RRSP funds at any one time. If you are age 65 or older, RRSP retirement income qualifies for the pension income tax credit. See Chapter 16.

RRSP Annuities

There are essentially two types of annuities—life and term-certain. Under a life annuity, the periodic payments, which you must receive at least once a year, continue until you die. The amount payable is based on factors that include the average life expectancy for someone your age and on current interest rates. Term-certain RRSP annuities are payable to age 90, or to the year your spouse turns age 90. Payments cease after your ninetieth year and are based primarily on current interest rates.

The table below illustrates the monthly income that a $50,000 investment will produce when invested in various ways at particular ages. The figures were supplied by Polson Bourbonniere Financial, a Toronto-based RRIF/annuity broker.

Monthly incomes shown commence one month after the purchase date. The listed incomes are subject to change as interest rates fluctuate, and represent an average of the highest-yielding plans at September 11, 1998.

Comparison of Monthly Income from a $50,000 Investment

| Age at Purchase | Single Life Annuity (10-Year Guarantee) | | Joint Life Annuity (10-Year Guarantee) | Term-Certain to Age 90 | RRIF (First Year's Income Only) |
	Male	Female	Male and Female	Male and Female	Minimum Payout
60	$331	$305	$286	$282	$139
61	336	309	289	285	144
62	342	314	293	289	149
63	348	319	297	294	154
64	354	324	302	298	160
65	361	330	307	305	167
66	368	335	312	311	174
67	375	342	317	317	181
68	383	348	323	324	189
69	390	355	330	331	198
70	398	363	336	340	208
71	408	370	343	348	308

When considering your retirement income options, remember that payments in the early years for indexed annuities are considerably lower than those for level payment annuities. They are much higher in later years, however, when you might require a higher income to cover increased health care costs. Carefully assess your income requirements over the long term before committing yourself to any of the options.

Registered Retirement Income Funds (RRIFs)

RRIFs have a number of advantages over annuities:

- Because you can determine the size of your annual payments to some extent, the inflation protection factor can be better controlled than with indexed annuities.
- Unusual income requirements in any year can be taken care of because you can withdraw any amount from a RRIF at any time, provided you withdraw at least the minimum amount.
- You can control the investments made in the RRIF, which generate the retirement income. (Of course, bad or risky investing could also dissipate your RRIF funds.)
- Your estate benefits because substantial amounts can remain in the RRIF, especially during the early years of its existence.
- You can convert amounts in a RRIF to a life annuity at any time, but the conversion cannot be reversed unless the life annuity is purchased through an RRSP and you are under age 69.

A RRIF resembles an RRSP. Funds are invested by the issuer, or the RRIF can be self-directed. Different plans may hold different types of eligible investments, which are similar to those allowed for RRSPs. All amounts in a RRIF remain tax-sheltered until paid out, and, as with an RRSP, investment performance affects the overall value of the plan.

A minimum amount must be paid out from each RRIF each year to the annuitant and be included in the annuitant's income for tax purposes. Since 1992, RRIF withdrawals can continue for the lifetime of the RRIF holder (or his or her spouse), instead of ceasing at age 90.

The table below compares the newer minimum withdrawal percentages to those under the former rules.

Comparison of Minimum Annual Withdrawals (% of RRIF Assets)

Age	Former Rules[1] (%)	Current Rules % General	Qualifying RRIFs[2]
71	5.26	7.38	5.26
72	5.56	7.48	5.56
73	5.88	7.59	5.88
74	6.25	7.71	6.25
75	6.67	7.85	6.67
76	7.14	7.99	7.14
77	7.69	8.15	7.69
78	8.33	8.33	8.33
79	9.09	8.53	8.53
80	10.00	8.75	8.75
81	11.11	8.99	8.99
82	12.50	9.27	9.27
83	14.29	9.58	9.58
84	16.67	9.93	9.93
85	20.00	10.33	10.33
86	25.00	10.79	10.79
87	33.33	11.33	11.33
88	50.00	11.96	11.96
89	100.00	12.71	12.71
90	N/A	13.62	13.62
91	N/A	14.73	14.73
92	N/A	16.12	16.12
93	N/A	17.92	17.92
94 or older	N/A	20.00	20.00

[1] The factors in this column are equal to $1/(90 - X)$, where X is the age of the annuitant or the annuitant's spouse, as the case may be.
[2] Defined as pre-1992 RRIFs.

The current rules apply to all RRIFs created after the end of 1992. For most RRIFs purchased before the end of 1992, or consisting exclusively of funds transferred from pre-1992 RRIFs ("qualifying RRIFs"), the previous minimum payment percentages will continue to apply for those up to age 77. The lower minimum payment percentages for those above age 78 will apply to all RRIFs entered into after March 1986 and pre-April 1986 RRIFs that have been amended.

At any point, you may withdraw any amount from any or all of your RRIFs, provided that you withdraw at least the minimum amount from each RRIF each year.

 Caution: By withdrawing large amounts, you will be reducing the size of payments in future years.

Withholding tax is payable on any excess withdrawn over the minimum amount that must be withdrawn in the year. The tax withheld becomes a credit against your tax payable for the year.

The surviving spouse of a RRIF annuitant who dies after 1990 becomes the annuitant under the fund under one of two conditions: either the parties must have previously agreed to the ongoing payments, or the legal representative of the first annuitant consents and the carrier of the fund undertakes to make payments to the surviving spouse. Payments will then continue to the spouse, and will be taxable in the spouse's hands only as each payment is received.

Collapsing Your RRSP

Although you can choose to collapse your RRSP, this is the default option if you do not make a choice for your RRSP before you turn 69. The tax consequences of this option should provide an incentive for you to create a maturity plan. If you collapse an RRSP, the entire amount in the plan must be brought into income and taxed in that year, often at the highest personal tax rate (see "Withdrawals from an RRSP" above).

If your retirement plans include moving to a foreign country and thus becoming a non-resident of Canada, you may be able to save on Canadian taxes by first establishing your non-resident status and then collapsing your RRSP. Non-resident withholding tax will apply to the funds withdrawn from your RRSP. This is likely to be at a lower rate than the rates for residents of Canada, particularly if you become a resident of a country with which Canada has a tax treaty providing for a specially reduced rate of withholding. For example, the withholding rate for periodic RRSP withdrawals under the Canada–U.S. Tax Convention is 15 per cent, compared with the regular 25 per cent.

There is no withholding of provincial tax if you are a non-resident and have collapsed your RRSP after you ceased being a Canadian resident.

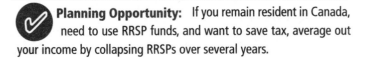

Planning Opportunity: If you remain resident in Canada, need to use RRSP funds, and want to save tax, average out your income by collapsing RRSPs over several years.

With only three tax brackets, however, the maximum tax rate is difficult to avoid. Not everyone will save tax by collapsing RRSPs over several years.

Apart from paying tax at a high marginal rate when you collapse an RRSP, you also lose the tax deferral still available in the RRSP, a RRIF, or even an annuity. Of course, tax deferral is probably of little concern if the RRSP is collapsed to satisfy immediate cash requirements.

The major advantage of collapsing an RRSP is that funds can be made available in an amount to suit your needs in the early years of retirement. There does not even have to be an excessive tax cost if you are under age 69 and do not mature your other RRSPs until you absolutely must. A similar result can be achieved, however, with a RRIF and it can be done at lower cost and more easily.

If You Drive a Car for Business

ʻ

This chapter highlights the principal tax rules affecting the business use of automobiles. In view of the complexity of these rules, you should still seek professional advice to deal adequately with your specific situations.

TAX ASPECTS FOR EMPLOYEES: EMPLOYEE-PROVIDED VEHICLES

Allowances and Reimbursements You Receive

If you own your own vehicle, your company may compensate you for the time you use the vehicle for business or for personal purposes.

One approach is for your employer to pay you an "automobile allowance." This allowance may be calculated to cover only the business-related costs of owning and operating the vehicle. Alternatively, it may be part of your total remuneration package, thereby covering more than just business-related costs.

Allowances are reported by your employer to Revenue Canada in one of two ways. First, if the allowance is not a reasonable amount for business-related purposes computed on the basis of kilometres driven, it must be reported on your T4 slip as employment income for the year.

As you would expect, Revenue Canada sets the standard for what qualifies as a reasonable rate. If your allowance is not reasonable, you can still generally deduct a portion of the expenses incurred if you operate the vehicle for business use. To qualify for a deduction, you must be required by contract to use the vehicle in the course of your employment, among other criteria.

Employers must also add the 7 per cent GST (and the 7.5 per cent Quebec Sales Tax (QST), if applicable) to the taxable benefit resulting from the vehicle allowance.

Second, if the employer pays you for business use, and if the amount is a reasonable allowance for that purpose, the employer should not report this allowance as part of your taxable income. An allowance will be considered "reasonable" only if it is directly related to the number of business kilometres driven in a year and if no reimbursement is received for expenses related to the same use.

To establish that there is a direct relation between the allowance and the business kilometres driven, you may be expected to provide your employer with detailed records of your business driving distances. If you are reimbursed for the cost of additional commercial insurance for the vehicle, parking, tolls, and ferries, your allowance may still be considered reasonable provided that the allowance is determined without reference to these expenses.

The *Income Tax Act* sets a prescribed rate for what is considered a reasonable per-kilometre allowance. Your employer is entitled to deduct allowances paid to employees at the prescribed rate. (The prescribed rates for 1998 are 35 cents on the first 5,000 kilometres and 29 cents for additional kilometres.) Provided that the rate still qualifies as reasonable, your employer may pay you at a higher rate without reporting it as taxable income to you. Your employer will probably not pay you above the prescribed rate because your employer's deduction is limited by the rate. It is unlikely that your employer would be willing to incur a non-deductible expense. In any event, you should keep records to indicate the cost of operating your car in case you are called on to support the allowance.

The second choice for the allowance is to have it treated as taxable remuneration. If this is done, you will be permitted to deduct at least a portion of the costs of operating the vehicle for business purposes if you meet all the criteria. In many circumstances, this may be to your advantage. Moreover, you may be able to claim GST (and QST) rebates on your deductible expenses. For more details, see Chapter 5.

Specific reimbursements of direct costs incurred in the operation of your vehicle in your employer's business (e.g., gas related to identifiable business travel) are not allowances and are not considered in calculating your taxable income.

Deducting Expenses from Your Income

Eligibility. You may be allowed to claim various deductions for the ownership and operating costs of your vehicle related to its use in the course of your employment. To be eligible for these deductions, you must not receive a tax-free allowance and you must be required by your terms of employment (technically your contract of employment, which need not be written) to pay your own travel expenses. You also must be required to work away from your employer's place of business or in different places on a regular basis. A prescribed form (T2200 for federal purposes and TP-64.3 in Quebec) must be signed by your employer to confirm that these conditions have been met, and it must be filed with your tax return.

If you claim expenses, any payment received from your employer to cover the costs of ownership of the vehicle will be a taxable allowance. Further, any reimbursement of operating expenses by your employer must be subtracted from any deduction claimed for the same expense.

Salespeople who sell property or negotiate contracts for their employers, and who are remunerated by commissions based on the volume of sales made or the contracts negotiated, may deduct part of their vehicle and other expenses. The deduction claim is limited to the amount of earned commissions, unless travelling expenses are the only type of expenses being claimed.

If you qualify to deduct vehicle expenses, you may deduct the business portion of the actual costs of ownership and operation, subject to the limitations discussed below for vehicles costing more than $26,000.

Deductions for Owned Vehicles

If you own the vehicle you use for business purposes, you are permitted capital cost allowance (CCA). CCA is the rate at which the capital costs of your vehicle can be written off against other income. CCA can be claimed on the total cost, but cannot exceed the applicable "maximum prescribed cost." According to the *Income Tax Act*, the maximum prescribed costs for vehicles acquired:

- after December 31, 1997: $26,000 plus GST and provincial sales tax;
- for prior acquisitions:

Acquisition date	Limit on cost	
June 18/87-Aug. 31/89	$20,000	
Sept. 1/89-Dec. 31/90	$24,000	
1991-1996	$24,000	plus GST & PST
1997	$25,000	plus GST & PST

If you acquired the car from a non-arm's length person (i.e., a related person), the cost for CCA purposes is adjusted. The adjusted cost will be the least of the maximum prescribed cost (as set out above), fair market value immediately before the disposition, and the transferor's undepreciated capital cost (UCC) immediately before the disposition (i.e., the amount not yet claimed as CCA).

When you sell the vehicle, the terminal loss and recapture rules do not apply if the cost was in excess of the maximum prescribed cost. The result is that no recapture of CCA (i.e., no addition to taxable income) or no deduction of a terminal loss is allowed, depending on whether you sold the vehicle for a profit or loss, respectively.

For CCA purposes, the cost of each car that is less than $26,000 is included in class 10 in the Regulations under the *Income Tax Act*. This means that the rate of depreciation for CCA purposes is 30 per cent (15 per cent in the year of acquisition) on a declining balance basis.

When the cost of a car, without the applicable taxes, is $26,000 or more, it is included in a separate pool within class 10.1. The rate of depreciation for CCA purposes for a class 10.1 vehicle is also 30 per cent (15 per cent in the year of acquisition) on a declining balance basis. The difference is that you may also claim CCA at 15 per cent in the year of disposition of a class 10.1 vehicle.

For example, if the cost of your car purchased on October 1, 1998, is $35,000, because of the half-year rule, applicable in the first year of ownership, you may claim 15 per cent of the maximum prescribed cost (based on the maximum of $26,000 plus 15 per cent PST and GST, the claim would be $4,485) in that year. In the second year and the following years, you may claim 30 per cent of the excess of the maximum prescribed cost over CCA previously claimed (or $7,624 in the second year). In the year in which the vehicle is sold, you will not own the vehicle at year-end and no CCA can be claimed. The special rule for class 10.1 vehicles allows that one-half of the depreciation (CCA) that would have been allowed in the year of sale if the vehicle were still owned at year-end is deductible.

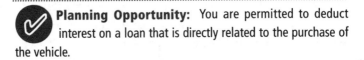

Planning Opportunity: You are permitted to deduct interest on a loan that is directly related to the purchase of the vehicle.

The interest deduction is limited to a maximum average of $250 per month after 1996 ($300 from September 1, 1989, to December 31, 1996, and $250 for vehicles acquired before September 1, 1989) for the period that the loan is outstanding.

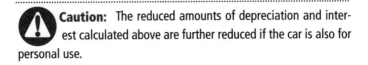

Caution: The reduced amounts of depreciation and interest calculated above are further reduced if the car is also for personal use.

Deductions for Leased Vehicles

If you lease your car, you may deduct the least of:

• the actual lease cost;

• $650 per month plus GST and applicable provincial sales tax for leases entered into after 1997; for prior leases:

Lease Date	Limit on monthly lease expense
June 18/87-Aug. 31/89	$600
Sept. 1/89-Dec. 31/96	$650
Jan. 1/97-Dec. 31/97	$550

• the actual lease cost multiplied by the maximum prescribed amount (including GST and the applicable provincial sales tax) and divided by 85 per cent of the manufacturer's suggested list price. For leases entered into before 1991, provincial sales tax must be added to the suggested list price.

> **Caution:** Revenue Canada considers a lease down payment (typical of most of today's lease arrangements) as a buydown of the monthly lease payments. The buydown must be considered in the above calculation.

For example, for an Ontario resident, if your car's manufacturer's suggested list price is $44,000 and the monthly lease payment under a lease entered into on October 1, 1998, is $950, the three alternatives will be $950, $747 ($650 × 1.15; GST 7% plus PST 8%), and $760 ($950 × $29,900/85 per cent of $44,000). Therefore, the maximum deduction will be $747. This example is not necessarily representative of the circumstances that will apply to this price range of car.

Reductions for Personal Use

Deductible ownership or lease costs as calculated above are further reduced because you must multiply them by the ratio of business kilometres to total kilometres.

Your deduction for operating costs (fuel, repairs, and maintenance) is also limited in the same proportion. The same rule holds true when calculating your eligible GST rebate or QST rebate (for repairs and maintenance only).

Purchase Assistance

Your employer may be willing to assist you in the purchase of your car, for example, by providing you with an interest-free (or low-interest) loan. In this case, any reduction in interest below the government-prescribed rate of interest (set every quarter) is considered a taxable benefit. Accordingly, your taxable earnings are increased by the amount of the loan outstanding multiplied by the prescribed interest rate for the period the loan is outstanding. Any interest that you pay to your employer is considered an expense, however, and you may deduct a portion of the deemed interest payment. Recall that the maximum interest deduction on a loan is an average of $250 per month for vehicles purchased after 1996.

Because you probably would have paid more than the prescribed rate if you had borrowed the money from a bank, but the cost to the employer (including lost investment income) is likely to approximate the prescribed rate, a loan from your employer may be one of the best ways of receiving a real benefit at a relatively low tax cost.

TAX ASPECTS FOR EMPLOYEES: COMPANY-PROVIDED VEHICLES

If your company provides you with a car, you could be required to include several amounts in taxable income. These amounts include a standby charge (a notional charge for making the car available to you), any benefit you receive for operating expenses paid by your employer for personal use, and taxable allowances. As mentioned earlier, the value of the benefits added to your income is subject to GST (and QST, if applicable), which is payable by your employer. Employers are required to report the GST (and QST, if applicable) as a taxable benefit on their employees' T4s (Relevé 1 in Quebec).

Specific reimbursement of out-of-pocket expenses (gasoline, parking, etc.) directly related to business use is not included as a taxable benefit. It is to your advantage to understand how your employer calculates the taxable amount. In some cases (and assuming you have a choice), you may prefer to own your own vehicle and receive an allowance, rather than using a car provided by your employer.

Standby Charge

You must include in your taxable income a "standby charge," a rough measure of the benefit to you of having the car available for personal use. This charge is calculated differently depending on whether the car is owned or leased by your employer.

Owned Vehicles. If the vehicle is owned by your employer, the standby charge is 2 per cent of the original cost of the car (including GST and provincial sales tax) for each month the car is available to you (24 per cent for a full year). This 2 per cent is calculated on the full cost of the car, regardless of whether this cost is in excess of the maximum prescribed cost.

Planning Opportunity: This standby charge may be reduced if you use the car all or substantially all for business (interpreted by Revenue Canada as 90 per cent or more) and your personal use is under 1,000 kilometres per month.

In this case, the standby charge is calculated as follows:

$$
\begin{array}{c}
\text{Standby charge} \\
\text{otherwise} \\
\text{calculated}
\end{array}
\times
\dfrac{\text{kilometres for personal use in the year}}{1{,}000 \times \text{number of months in the year in which the car is available to the employee}}
$$

For example, if your personal use is only 200 kilometres per month and equivalent to 5 per cent of the total use, you will be taxable on only 20 per cent (2,400 km/12,000 km) of the standby charge otherwise calculated. Commuting to your employer's office is considered personal (not business) use of the car.

An optional method is available for calculating the standby charge if you are employed principally in selling new or used cars.

The standby rules apply to members of a partnership as if they were employees.

Leased Vehicles. The standby charge included in your income for vehicles leased by your employer is two-thirds of the lease cost (including GST and provincial sales tax) and any amount included in the lease cost for repairs and maintenance, but excluding any amount included for insurance. The insurance amount is included in operating costs for the purpose of determining any operating benefit, but is excluded to establish the benefit resulting from GST and QST, if applicable. This standby charge is calculated on the full lease cost paid by your employer, whether or not the amount in respect of which your employer may claim deductions is the full cost.

It may be better for you if your employer leases the car rather than owns it. Two-thirds of the annual lease payment may work out to less than 24 per cent of the cost that would be chargeable if the employer owned the vehicle. There is also greater flexibility in a lease. Specifically, some service costs can be included in the lease contract. The result is that the value of these services will be taxable benefits to you only to the extent of two-thirds of the lease cost.

If your personal use amounts to less than 10 per cent of time driven and less than 1,000 kilometres per month, this standby charge also may be reduced as discussed under "Owned Vehicles" above.

Reimbursements to Your Employer

If you reimburse your employer for part of the cost of the vehicle, the standby charge otherwise included in your income is reduced by the amount of that reimbursement. This reduction offers you an advantage if your employer leases the vehicle. You can deduct your full lease payment against an amount that is only two-thirds of the lease cost. While you may receive a tax benefit, a reimbursement is a tax liability for your employer. Consequently, your employer may be reluctant to permit such an arrangement.

Other Ownership and Operating Expenses

When your employer also pays for such items as insurance, licence, fuel, and repairs and maintenance, you may have an additional taxable benefit. The benefit is equivalent to 14 cents per personal kilometre driven after 1996 (13 cents per personal kilometre driven prior to 1997), including 0.65 cents for the GST. The 14 cents per kilometre rate may also be used for Quebec tax purposes and includes the GST and the Quebec Sales Tax. The rate is periodically revised.

Election in Respect of Operating Expenses

As an alternative to calculating your taxable benefit at a rate of 14 cents per personal kilometre (11 cents per kilometre for automobile salespeople), you can make an election based on the operating expenses. If you use the car primarily for business, you can elect to include in income an amount equal to one-half of the standby charge. In this context, "primarily for business" means more than 50 per cent. If you elect to use this method, you must notify your employer in writing before the end of the applicable year that you are making the election.

Shareholders

The same rules for employee automobile benefits generally apply to a shareholder of a corporation.

TAX ASPECTS FOR EMPLOYERS AND SELF-EMPLOYED INDIVIDUALS

Allowances

A reasonable allowance paid to an employee for business purposes and based on the number of business kilometres driven in the year is not included in the employee's income. To lessen the administrative difficulty of maintaining mileage records for each employee on a regular basis, Revenue Canada will allow a tax-free fixed allowance to be paid to an employee during the year provided the following conditions exist:

- There is a pre-established per-kilometre rate.
- The rate and the advance are reasonable.
- At the earlier of the calendar year-end or the date the employee ceases to be employed, the actual kilometres travelled for business purposes are calculated. If the employer has overpaid, the employee must refund the excess to the employer. If the employee was underpaid, the employer must make up the difference.
- The employee is not required to include the amount in income under any other provision of the *Income Tax Act*.

Deductible Expenditures

If your employees use their own cars for business, you may deduct certain allowances or reimbursements you pay them in respect of the business use. In addition, you are eligible for an input tax credit for GST paid on employee-reimbursed expenditures and the GST deemed to be included in the amount of paid allowances. For QST purposes, you are also eligible for the credit for expenditures on which the QST is actually paid and on which the QST is deemed to be included in the amount of paid allowances. This eligibility may not apply to large businesses (i.e., those with $6 million or more of gross income).

If you provide cars to your employees, your deductible amounts are limited to non-capital, "reasonable" expenses incurred for the purpose of earning income from a business, profession, or property. Accordingly, you may deduct all leasing or ownership costs up to the maximum amounts set out above, and reasonable operating costs, parking costs, and so forth for the vehicles provided. You also may deduct interest expense incurred on debt used to purchase the vehicles. The interest expense deduction limit for money borrowed to purchase an automobile is:

Acquisition date	Limit on monthly interest
June 18/87-Aug. 31/89	$250
Sept. 1/89-Dec. 31/96	$300
Jan. 1/1997 and after	$250

Employer Deductions in Respect of Employee-Provided Vehicles

As an employer, you can deduct certain distance-based car allowances paid to an employee in respect of the use of his or her car for the benefit of your business, even when these are not reported as taxable income of the employee. You may fully deduct any car allowances or similar payments that are reported on the employee's T4 as fully taxable.

You will be permitted to deduct tax-free allowances to an employee to the extent that they do not exceed, for 1997 onward, 35 cents for each of the first 5,000 business kilometres driven by the employee in a year, and 29 cents for each additional business kilometre. An additional four cents per kilometre is allowed in Yukon and the Northwest Territories.

You may deduct payments made regarding fuel, maintenance, and repairs in full, although the part of these costs related to personal use of the car will be taxable income to the employee.

Employer Deductions in Respect of Company-Provided Vehicles

If your company purchases or leases vehicles that are provided to employees, you will be required to calculate a standby charge, as discussed above, and include the taxable benefit on your employees' T4s (Relevé 1 in Quebec). Although you are required to pay GST and QST (from 1996 for small businesses and from 1998 for large corporations) on the benefit, you may be able to claim the GST and the QST on the purchase price or the lease cost of the car, subject to the maximum amounts prescribed.

Company-Owned Vehicles

Your company is permitted regular capital cost allowance (CCA) deductions for vehicles that it owns and that are used in business. Existing CCA rules apply to vehicles costing the maximum prescribed cost, or less. The vehicles will be included in the current CCA class 10, which allows a 30 per cent CCA rate. Current recapture, half-year, terminal loss, and pooling rules continue to apply for cars meeting the criteria described above.

If you purchase a car costing in excess of the maximum prescribed cost, each car must be included in a separate CCA class 10.1. The other tax measures for employees described above in the section "Deductions for Owned Vehicles" also apply to employers.

Leased Vehicles

If your company provides leased vehicles to its employees, the maximum deduction regarding the lease cost is the same as the deduction available to individuals, as described above. To prevent indirect increases to the maximum allowable deduction, the *Income Tax Act* rules prevent your company from making refundable payments to the lessor for the purpose of reducing the monthly amount of rent.

If you provide your employees with leased vehicles, any reimbursement by an employee of your lease expense will reduce the deductible portion of your cost. This can have a very punitive effect in the case of luxury cars. For example, if you pay $1,800 per month for a lease entered into on October 1, 1998, your maximum deduction before any reimbursement totals $747 (for an Ontario resident). If the employee reimbursement is $747 or greater, you obtain no deduction. If the reimbursement is less than $747, it must be deducted from the $747 allowable deduction.

PLANNING FOR BUSINESS USE OF AUTOMOBILES

In most cases, review existing policies and available alternatives to maximize tax deductions and the benefits to employees. In addition, don't ignore the ramifications of the Goods and Services Tax.

In light of these factors, consider the following options:

- an interest-free loan instead of a car allowance or a company car;
- having the employer provide a leased car instead of a purchased car;
- leasing the car initially and purchasing it at a later date; or
- having a car available to you that is used exclusively, or at least 90 per cent, for business.

Consult your professional advisor to discuss the tax consequences of particular approaches and pick the one that suits your situation.

If You Are a Senior

THE TAXATION OF SENIORS

This chapter highlights the government benefits, credits, and deductions available to seniors. For information on your RRSP, maturity options, and taxation of retirement income, refer to Chapter 14.

Income in the Form of Benefits

If you have worked in Canada and made contributions to the Canada or Quebec Pension Plan (CPP/QPP), you are likely entitled to apply for your pension benefits from those plans. You can begin collecting your CPP benefits at any age between 60 and 70. If you delay collecting your benefits after age 65, your eligible benefits will be increased to a maximum of 130 per cent (at 6 per cent per year). CPP benefits are included in your taxable income for the year they are received.

If you have been a resident for at least 10 years after reaching age 18, you also may qualify to apply for Old Age Security

(OAS) benefits. Residency of at least 40 years after age 18, including the 10 years immediately preceding your application, qualifies you for full benefits. You need not have a work history in Canada to qualify for OAS. Your OAS pension benefit is taxable income.

Planning Opportunity: You can apply to have your CPP benefits split between you and your spouse to reduce your taxable income. You must both be at least 60 years of age.

While the amount of your CPP/QPP benefits depends on how much you have contributed to the plan, they are not affected by the amount of your other retirement income. The OAS benefit is affected by how much you earn in retirement from other sources and has a built-in "clawback" mechanism. The OAS repayment is $0.15 for each dollar of individual net income over $53,215. For single seniors, OAS benefits are fully recovered if you earn (net) about $85,000. Because the OAS clawback is calculated on an individual basis, optimize opportunities to split your retirement income with your spouse. Also consider postponing the receipt of retirement income, including your CPP/QPP benefits, and continue to contribute to your RRSP until you are 69.

Planning Opportunity: Delay deducting your RRSP contributions in the last two years before retiring. You can carry forward your deductions and use them to reduce your future taxable income and also to reduce the OAS clawback.

Seniors Benefit Scrapped

In July 1998 the federal government announced that the proposed Seniors Benefit will not proceed. The existing OAS/GIS system will be fully maintained. (GIS is the Guaranteed Income Supplement.)

CREDITS AND DEDUCTIONS

Age 65 and Over

If you turn 65 before the end of 1998, you can claim a $592 federal tax credit. This credit is 17 per cent of the "age amount" ($3,482 currently). The age amount is reduced by 15 per cent of an individual's net income exceeding $25,921. You cannot claim this credit if you have an annual net income of $49,134 or more. If you are unable to make full use of the credit, all or a portion of it can be transferred to your spouse. The federal credit is indexed annually according to increases in the Consumer Price Index above 3 per cent.

Pension Income

If you turn 65 before the end of 1998, you can claim a maximum federal tax credit of $170 against your pension income, provided that the income is at least $1,000. If it is less than $1,000, the maximum credit is 17 per cent of the pension income. Payments from registered pension plans, a DPSP, an RRSP, or a RRIF will qualify as long as they are periodic payments, and not lump sum amounts.

A similar credit is available in respect of "qualified pension income" for taxpayers who are under 65 at the end of the year. Qualified pension income includes life annuity payments from a pension fund or plan and, conditionally, income that qualifies as pension income for individuals under age 65. You must be receiving the income as a result of the death of your spouse.

If you cannot make full use of your pension income tax credit, the unused portion may be transferred to your spouse. The pension income tax credit is not subject to indexing and therefore remains at the level at which it was introduced in 1988.

Mental or Physical Impairment

If you have a severe and prolonged mental or physical impairment that has been certified by a medical doctor, optometrist, audiologist, occupational therapist, or psychologist, you can claim a federal tax credit in 1998 of $720. This federal credit is indexed annually according to increases in the Consumer Price Index above 3 per cent. Any unused portion of the credit may, under certain circumstances, be transferred to a spouse or to another person who supported you.

The Medical Expense Credit—Specific Issues for Seniors

The medical expenses credit is available to all Canadians, but it has specific relevance for Canadian seniors. Refer to Chapter 6 for detailed discussion of the qualifying amounts and services covered. In addition to those services, the following expenses can be claimed:

- costs related to artificial limbs, wheelchairs, crutches, hearing aids, prescription glasses or contact lenses, dentures, pacemakers, prescription drugs, and specified prescription medical devices;
- if you or a person you support lacks normal physical development or has a severe and prolonged mobility impairment, you can claim reasonable construction and equipment expenses associated with modifying your home to enable the individual to gain access to, or to be mobile or functional within, the home;
- guide and hearing-ear dogs, as well as signal equipment for your home if you have a hearing impairment;
- most premiums paid to a private health insurance plan; and
- rehabilitation therapy costs for individuals with speech or hearing loss.

In addition, if the required medical treatment is not available within a commuting distance from your home, you may be able to claim reasonable travelling expenses.

If you claim medical expenses for yourself or your spouse and either of you requires attendant care or care in an establishment, you may be eligible to claim those costs. Qualifying costs include full- or part-time attendant care and will be included in your medical expenses claim. Generally if you claim full-time attendant care as part of your medical expenses, you cannot also claim the mental or physical impairment credit discussed above. However, if the cost of attendant care does not exceed $10,000, you can also claim the mental or physical impairment credit.

If You Provide Care for Your Parents

N umerous Canadians provide support for their elderly parents or grandparents. The government is recognizing that this added responsibility results in added costs. The credits and deductions described here are available to allay some of those expenses. Some of these credits extend beyond assisting Canadians caring for elderly parents. With the exception of the equivalent-to-spouse and the caregiver tax credits, the credits and deductions listed here are available to individuals providing care to a relative or spouse suffering a physical or mental impairment.

CREDITS AND DEDUCTIONS

Equivalent-to-Spouse

You can qualify for the equivalent-to-spouse tax credit if you support a wholly dependent person and are unmarried, or are married but did not support or live with your spouse. The federal credit is $915 in 1998, reduced by 17 per cent of the dependant's income over $538. If the dependant's income is $5,918 or more, the credit is nil.

To claim the credit, you must maintain a "self-contained domestic establishment in which you live with and support the dependant." You can do this on your own or with others (e.g., your siblings can assist you in the care of your elderly parent).

The dependant must be related to you, wholly dependent on you (or on you and certain others) for support, and must be resident in Canada, unless the dependant is your child. Except in the case of a parent or grandparent, the dependant must be either under 18 years of age at any time in the year or dependent by reason of mental or physical infirmity.

You can claim this credit in respect of only one other person, and no more than one individual can claim the credit for the same person or the same self-contained domestic establishment. If you and another person are both eligible to claim the credit for the same dependant or the same self-contained domestic establishment, you must agree between yourselves who will make the claim. In the absence of agreement, the credit will apparently not be allowed to anybody.

If you are entitled to claim the equivalent-to-spouse credit in respect of a person, neither you nor anyone else may claim a dependant tax credit in respect of that person. The equivalent-to-spouse federal tax credit is indexed annually according to increases in the Consumer Price Index above 3 per cent.

NEW **New for 1998!** The 1998 federal budget proposed a supplement of $500 to the equivalent-to-spouse credit for low-income earners. The increase will be implemented by way of a supplementary non-refundable amount calculated separately on your tax return. For 1998, the credit is effective in July. The credit is reduced by 17 per cent of the dependant's income in excess of $6,956.

Dependants

If your parent does not live with you, or if you are married, you might be eligible to claim the dependant credit if your parent meets the qualification of suffering from a mental or physical impairment. A "dependant" can include a child or grandchild of you or your spouse or, if resident in Canada at any time in the year, a parent, grandparent, brother, sister, uncle, aunt, niece, or nephew of you or your spouse.

If a dependant is claimed under the equivalent-to-spouse tax credit described above, that person cannot also be claimed as a dependant with a mental or physical infirmity. Details on the dependant credit are contained in Chapter 13.

If you and another person or persons are entitled to claim a dependant tax credit in respect of the same dependant, the total claimed cannot exceed the maximum allowed for one individual making the claim. Revenue Canada may allocate the total tax credit to the supporting individuals if they cannot agree on an allocation.

Mental or Physical Impairment

If the person with a qualifying severe and prolonged mental or physical impairment cannot use all of this credit, any unused portion of the credit may, under certain circumstances, be transferred to a spouse or to another person who supported the individual. See Chapter 13 for details.

Caregiver Tax Credit

NEW **New for 1998!** If the equivalent-to-spouse or dependant tax credit has not been claimed in respect of a dependant by any person, you may be eligible to claim the new credit. The caregiver tax credit can reduce federal tax up to a maximum of $400 for individuals who live with and provide in-home care for a parent or grandparent (including in-laws) over the age of 65 or a dependent relative who has a mental or physical infirmity. The credit is reduced proportionately by the dependant's net income over $11,500.

Medical Expense Tax Credit

New for 1998! Also new for 1998 is the addition to the list of allowable medical expenses of reasonable expenses for training an individual to care for a relative who has a mental or physical infirmity. The relative must live with or be dependent on you for support.

CHAPTER EIGHTEEN

If You Make Political or Charitable Contributions

Although these charitable donations and political contributions credits are in place to encourage Canadians to make gifts and contributions to aid a public purpose, the requirements and conditions are confusing. Making a contribution requires planning, and you must consider both the amount and the timing of your gift to maximize your tax benefit.

CREDITS AND DEDUCTIONS

Charitable Donations

The federal tax credit on qualifying charitable donations is 17 per cent on the first $200 donated and 29 per cent on donations above $200. For an individual in the top tax bracket (assuming a 55 per cent rate of provincial tax), the total credit on a $1,000 donation in 1998 will be about $434:

Calculation of the Charitable Donations Credit

Federal credit at 17% on first $200 donated	$ 34.00
Federal credit at 29% on excess ($800)	232.00
Total federal credits	266.00
Surtax reduction	21.28
	287.28
Provincial tax reduction at 55% of $266	146.30
Total tax reduction	$433.58

Any donation not claimed under the tax credit system in a given year can be carried forward for five years. In the carryforward year, however, the 17 per cent rate applies to the first $200 of all donations claimed, including carryforward donations. A deferral may result in a small tax cost if your donation falls short of $200 that year, but would have been part of a larger gift in another year.

The annual limit on qualifying donations to both charitable institutions and the Crown is 75 per cent of net income. Where appreciated capital property is gifted, the 75 per cent limit is further increased by one-quarter of the taxable gain arising from the gifted property. In this case, the donation limit would equal 100 per cent of the net income that arises as a consequence of the gift. Also, in the year of death and in the immediately preceding taxation year, the limit on gifts, including bequests or legacies, is 100 per cent of the individual's net income.

As another incentive to encourage charitable gifting, the tax you will pay on any gain realized in the gift of publicly traded securities to a charity is half the normal rate, or 37.5 per cent. If you donate shares to a charity and recognize a capital gain, only 37.5 per cent of that gain is added to your taxable income for the year of the donation. This measure is specifically limited to publicly traded securities and is effective for gifts made after February 18, 1997, and before 2002.

The following chart shows the benefit of using this provision:

Comparison of Charitable Gift Benefit for Various Gifts[1]

	Sale of Shares & Gift of Cash	Gift of Shares (Old Rule)	Gift of Shares (New Rule)	Gift of Cash
Value of Gift	$610	$1,000	$1,000	$1,000
Tax Relief of Gift	(320)	(520)	(520)	(520)
Tax on Capital Gain	390	390	195	–
Cost to Donor	$680	$ 870	$ 675	$ 480

[1] The amounts shown in the table do not apply in Quebec.

Planning Opportunity: Pool the credit. Claiming a donation of $400 on one spouse's return (rather than each spouse claiming $200) saves tax because half the donation qualifies for the 29 per cent federal rate rather than the 17 per cent rate.

Emergency Service Volunteer Allowances

New for 1998! If you donate your time as opposed to property, you may qualify for some added tax breaks in 1998. Specifically, if you are a volunteer fire-fighter, your tax-free allowance is now $1,000, up from $500. This change is effective January 1, 1998, and the increased allowance is extended to other qualifying emergency service volunteers. The $1,000 allowance will be reduced proportionately by the amount of compensation you receive in excess of $3,000 for your services.

Political Contributions

A federal tax credit is available for contributions to a registered political party or an officially nominated candidate in a federal election. The credit is based on the amount contributed and is calculated on a sliding scale. The maximum credit for any one taxation year is $500.

Comparison of Credit Available for Various Amounts of Gifts

Amount Contributed	Tax Credit Available
$1–$100	75% of the contribution
$100–$550	$75 plus 50% of excess over $100
$550–$1,150	$300 plus one-third of excess over $550
Over $1,150	$500

All provinces and territories except Saskatchewan also permit tax credits for political contributions, but the credit is deducted from provincial tax payable and contributions must be made to provincial political parties or associations, or to candidates standing for provincial election.

The tax credit in British Columbia, Manitoba, Newfoundland, Nova Scotia, New Brunswick, Prince Edward Island, and the Yukon Territory is calculated in the same manner as for federal purposes, and the maximum credit is $500. In the Northwest Territories, the credit is 100 per cent of the first $100 contributed and 50 per cent of the excess over $100, to a maximum credit of $500. The maximum credit in Ontario is $750, calculated as 75 per cent of the first $200, 50 per cent of the next $600, and $33\frac{1}{3}$ per cent of the next $900. The maximum credit in Alberta is also $750, calculated as 75 per cent of the first $150 contributed, 50 per cent of the next $675, and $33\frac{1}{3}$ per cent of the next $900. In Quebec, the tax credit is calculated as 75 per cent of the first $200 contributed and 50 per cent of the next $200, to a maximum of $250.

Official receipts must be filed with your tax return to receive the credit. Generally, political contributions must be made in the form of cash or other negotiable instruments (cheques, money orders, etc.). However, some provinces permit the contribution of goods or services under certain conditions.

You cannot claim the credit for political contributions in excess of $1,150 ($900 in the Northwest Territories, $400 in Quebec, $1,725 in Alberta, and $1,700 in Ontario) in any one taxation year. If the tax credit exceeds your federal or provincial tax payable after the deduction of other credits, you cannot claim a refund of tax or carry forward any excess credit to a future taxation year.

Planning for Your Contributions. If you are making a large contribution, spread it over two years. You will be able to take advantage of the larger credits available. For example, if you contribute $1,000 in one year, your credit is $450 (except in the Northwest Territories, Quebec, Ontario, and Alberta). If you contribute $500 this year and $500 next year, your total credit is $550, giving you a $100 tax saving. This same technique should also be applied if both spouses earn taxable income, except that the spouses would split their contribution in the year (i.e., each spouse would contribute $500, instead of one spouse contributing $1,000). Splitting the contribution is beneficial because the maximum percentage credit applies at lower contribution levels.

If You Live in Quebec

A lthough the Quebec government has largely harmonized its tax legislation with the federal legislation, there are some differences, especially with the personal income tax credits. Details of these credit amounts and a few other features particular to the Quebec system are outlined in Chapter 20.

In addition, the Quebec government has tax benefits available to its residents that are offered concurrently by the federal government or are uniquely adapted to the economic needs of the province. They are designed to promote investments in strategic sectors of industry such as mining exploration, film production, scientific research, etc.

This chapter discusses certain specific tax measures that apply to Quebec residents.

CREDITS AND DEDUCTIONS

Employment Income

Quebec provides a tax credit of 23 per cent (20 per cent in 1997) for union and professional dues.

When employment duties are performed outside Canada in certain types of businesses (construction, engineering, etc.), federal legislation provides a tax credit, while Quebec legislation provides for a deduction in calculating taxable income. In both cases, similar conditions must be met in order to have access to these tax benefits.

Tuition Fees

When fees exceed $100, a tax credit equal to 17 per cent is allowed under the federal system. Where the credit is not fully claimed, it may be transferred to a spouse or parent to a maximum of $850.

Under Quebec legislation, tuition fees are eligible for a 23 per cent tax credit that can be claimed only by the student. Transfers to another taxpayer are not allowed. Moreover, examination fees charged by professional corporations mentioned in Schedule 1 of the Professional Code (i.e., exclusive professions and professions with reserved titles) are deductible when the examinations are required to become a member of one of the corporations or to practise one of the professions mentioned in the Schedule.

Child Care Expenses

Contrary to the federal legislation, which allows individuals to deduct child care expenses, the Quebec legislation provides a refundable tax credit for these expenses, based on family income, going from 26 per cent to 75 per cent. Most of the rules in both pieces of legislation are similar when it comes to determining eligible child care expenses.

Charitable Gifts

A taxpayer making a charitable gift is entitled to a tax credit, just as in the federal system, but the tax credit is different. Quebec legislation provides a flat 23 per cent (20 per cent before 1998) credit on the entire amount donated. The total amount of gifts that can be deducted in a given year is limited to 75 per cent (20 per cent before 1998) of net income. Since May 10, 1995, if the gift is a work of art, the tax credit is generally limited to the selling price of the work of art by the organization to which the gift is given. Moreover, the sale must take place before the end of the fifth calendar year following the year of the gift; otherwise, the tax benefit will be forfeited.

Other Items

Some items contained in the Quebec legislation do not have a federal equivalent.

For instance, a person who resides in Quebec on December 31 may be entitled to a real estate tax refund. This credit is available to both tenants and homeowners. The size of the credit depends on the individual's total income and that of the spouse, if applicable. It also depends on the aggregate of real estate taxes for the year. For 1998, the maximum credit has been set at $514.

Finally, low- and middle-income families are entitled to a tax reduction. It provides a reduction of income tax, but is not refundable. The amount of the reduction depends on the household's total income. For 1998, the maximum has been set at $1,195 per person or $1,500 for a couple with at least one dependent child. Single parents who do not share an independent dwelling with another adult are also entitled to a tax reduction of $1,195.

TAX INCENTIVES

Quebec Stock Savings Plan

In 1979, the Quebec government introduced the stock savings plan (QSSP) to promote stock investments in Quebec companies and reduce the tax burden on individuals residing in the province. Although the QSSP has undergone several adjustments over the years, most making it less attractive, it nevertheless remains an interesting method of tax planning if you are prepared to acquire shares on the stock market.

It is wise to keep in mind, however, that any tax benefit achieved with a QSSP may be offset by a decline of the market value of the shares. Consequently, even when shares qualify under the QSSP, the first criterion you should investigate before purchasing shares is still their potential yield and growth. To reduce the risk associated with this type of investment, you can invest through a stock savings plan investment group or investment fund. One of the advantages of these alternative forms of investment is that you will have a share in a more diversified stock portfolio without having to make a considerable investment.

Tax Benefit. If you are a Quebec resident at the close of the tax year and have acquired qualifying shares in a stock savings plan during the year, you may deduct the adjusted cost of these shares from your taxable income, to a maximum of 10 per cent of your total income. Your "total income" is the net income amount that appears on your provincial income tax return, less the capital gains exemption used during the year. Shares must have been acquired prior to the end of the tax year and be included in the stock savings plan before February 1 of the following year to be considered qualifying shares. The allowable deduction is restricted to the "adjusted cost" of your shares; that is, to the full cost of the shares, excluding the cost of borrowing, brokers' commissions, or safekeeping fees.

These shares must be issued by "growth corporations," which means corporations with assets between $2 million and $300 million ($250 million before April 1, 1998). Moreover, growth corporations can issue unsecured debentures or preferred shares that entitle the holders to a 50 per cent QSSP deduction. To meet the eligibility requirements, these securities must, in particular, be convertible at any time into common shares carrying voting rights under all circumstances, and they must be listed on the Montreal Exchange.

For example, you purchase shares of growth corporations for $3,000. In 1998, your net income is $50,000, and you realized a taxable capital gain of $10,000 on the sale of qualified small business corporation shares for which the capital gains exemption has been used. Your QSSP deduction will amount to the lesser of the following:

- Adjusted cost of shares
  $3,000 × 100% $ 3,000

- 10% of your total income
  10% × ($50,000 – $10,000) $ 4,000

Your deduction will therefore be $3,000.

Management fees for a QSSP and the cost of borrowing to purchase shares constitute financial expenses and are deductible annually.

Additional Deductions. Shares included in a QSSP entitle the holder to an additional 25 per cent deduction on the cost of the shares when they are acquired under an employee stock option plan. An employer may create a plan to encourage employees to acquire the shares issued by the employer corporation when it goes public. The plan must be available to all employees and executives with more than three months of service and who own less than 5 per cent of the capital stock of the corporation immediately prior to acquiring shares in the stock option plan.

Recovery of Deductions. At the end of the two subsequent calendar years, your stock portfolio must contain shares that have an adjusted cost equal to the amount for which you obtained a deduction. Should this not be the case, you will either have to include a portion or all of the deductions previously allowed in your income for the year in which this condition is not met, or reduce the amount of the deduction that you could otherwise claim during the year.

If, for example, in 1996 you acquired $1,000 of shares, which at the time entitled you to a deduction of 100 per cent, and you sell these shares in 1998, you must, before the end of 1998, acquire replacement shares with an adjusted cost of $1,000 so that the deduction you obtained will not be added to your income during 1998. You cannot, however, benefit from a new QSSP deduction for the replacement shares.

In addition to newly issued shares, replacement shares also include the shares of growth corporations that already entitle the holder to the QSSP deduction if they are purchased on the secondary market and listed by the Commission des valeurs mobilières du Québec.

Capital Gains and Dividends. Dividends received on shares in stock savings plans are treated like any other dividend received on shares. When the shares are sold, the capital gain or loss is calculated in the usual manner. The tax benefit received does not reduce the actual cost of the shares.

QSSPs versus RRSPs. Unlike the RRSP, which only allows income tax payments to be deferred, the QSSP offers a real tax saving. The RRSP does, however, reduce your immediate income tax at both the federal and provincial levels, while the QSSP deduction can be used only in Quebec.

A share in a QSSP cannot be included under another tax plan at the same time. However, you can contribute successively to your QSSP and RRSP using the same funds and, because the deadlines for contributions are different, obtain the QSSP and the RRSP deduction for the same year.

Whereas shares included in a QSSP must be acquired before year-end, it is possible to contribute to an RRSP during the first 60 days of the subsequent year. As a result, QSSP shares can be sold at the beginning of the year following the year of acquisition and the sale proceeds can be used to make a contribution to an RRSP. To avoid the recovery of deductions, QSSP shares must be replaced before the end of the year in which they are sold, unless the adjusted cost of shares held for over two years in your QSSP portfolio allows you to escape this rule. The double deduction is therefore only temporary, but may prove useful if you do not have sufficient liquid assets available at this time of the year.

Cooperative Investment Plan

To encourage investments in certain Quebec cooperatives, the provincial government introduced the Quebec Cooperative Investment Plan. This plan provides a deduction to an individual who acquires eligible securities issued by a qualified cooperative. This deduction is only available to a member or worker of the cooperative and to an employee of a partnership to which the qualified cooperative contributes more than 50 per cent of the income.

The deduction and a two-year holding period are calculated in the same manner as under the QSSP. The deduction is equal to 100 per cent of the cost of the securities purchased, but not exceeding 10 per cent of total income. The basic deduction is 125 per cent for units issued by small- and medium-sized cooperatives, i.e., those with assets of less than $25 million or equity of no more than $10 million.

When a cooperative sets up a "stock ownership plan" (a plan allowing employees and officers to acquire securities in their cooperative) similar to the one discussed in the "Quebec Stock Savings Plan" section, individuals who acquire such securities are entitled to an additional deduction of 25 per cent, for a total deduction of 150 per cent of the cost of the shares.

Quebec Business Investment Companies

A Quebec Business Investment Company (QBIC) is a private corporation whose primary activity is to acquire shares of other unrelated eligible private corporations, which operate in pre-scribed sectors. These sectors include manufacturing, tourism, export, or environmental protection in Quebec. QBICs, which can only be incorporated in Quebec, are an intermediate financing vehicle between eligible private corporations and investors. They are private and not listed on the stock market.

Tax Benefit. If you are a Quebec resident on December 31 of a tax year and purchase common shares of a QBIC, you can qualify to deduct 150 per cent (125 per cent before April 1, 1998) of your purchase price from your taxable income for Quebec income tax purposes. This deduction can be taken only when the QBIC invests the money to acquire common shares of an eligible corporation. (Before April 1, 1998, an additional 25 per cent deduction was allowed if the QBIC invested in small- or medium-sized businesses located outside main urban centres. Moreover, if the QBIC shares were acquired as part of an employee stock option plan to encourage employees to purchase shares of the employer corporation through a QBIC, another 25 per cent deduction was granted. Thus, the total deduction could reach 175 per cent.)

However, the deduction used in a given year must not exceed 30 per cent of your total income; any portion not claimed in a year due to this limit may be carried forward for five years.

Investments in a QBIC do not affect contribution limits to RRSPs and QSSPs. Unlike a QSSP, you are not required to keep your QBIC securities for at least two years. This is the responsibility of the QBIC. If a QBIC constitutes an "active business" and the other criteria prescribed by law are met, you can even benefit from the $500,000 capital gains exemption on the sale or disposal of these shares.

Mineral Exploration and Oil and Gas Sectors

The acquisition of flow-through shares, whether directly or through a limited partnership, enables the holder to benefit from tax breaks for Quebec income tax purposes.

A deduction of up to 175 per cent of surface mining exploration expenses incurred in Quebec may be allowed. An additional deduction of 25 per cent is also available after March 31, 1998, for such expenses incurred in northern Quebec. Moreover, a further exemption is granted with respect to the capital gain realized on the sale of flow-through shares, thereby enabling the holder to obtain tax breaks related to exploration.

CONSEQUENCES OF MARRIAGE BREAKDOWN

Family Patrimony

Married persons are subject to the rules on family patrimony. These relate to economic equality between spouses in the event that there is a partition of family patrimony, whether through separation, dissolution or annulment of a marriage, or death.

The partition of family patrimony may be accompanied by a partition of certain property between the spouses. Each spouse may claim a right to certain portions of the family property. A valuation is done on the basis of the total net value, not on the basis of individual property.

Property subject to partition includes the family's principal and secondary residences, household furniture, motor vehicles used for family travel, and the benefits accrued during the marriage under public or private retirement plans. Any of this property that has been acquired before or during the marriage by way of succession, legacy, or gift is excluded from the family patrimony.

In the case of tax and estate planning, a spouse who makes a bequest to the other spouse should consider the implications of the partition of family patrimony. In addition to the bequest, the spouse will be entitled to 50 per cent of the net value of the property that is part of the family patrimony.

CORPORATE TAX ISSUES

Corporations Operating in Quebec

Tax Rates. In Chapter 8, we discussed the tax as well as the planning advantages available through the incorporation of a business. It was mentioned that the tax structure varies depending on the province in which the income was earned, as well as on the type and amount of income.

Under Quebec legislation, the basic corporate rate is 16.25 per cent. Under the federal Act, active business income is subject to a tax reduction, the "small business deduction" (SBD) (see Chapter 8). Where a corporation claims the SBD in its federal tax return, a 10.5 per cent reduction is provided under the Quebec *Taxation Act*. Where active business income is not subject to the federal SBD, a reduction of 7.35 per cent is provided.

The following schedule summarizes the effective Quebec corporate income tax rates:

Comparison of Quebec Corporate Income Tax Rates

	Active Business Income		
	Eligible for SBD	Not Eligible for SBD	Other Income
Basic rate	16.25%	16.25%	16.25%
Deduction allowed	10.50	7.35	—
Effective rate	5.75%	8.90%	16.25%

Note: An additional surtax of 2.8 per cent applies on account of contributions to the Anti-Poverty Fund after November 26, 1997.

Exemptions for New Corporations. To stimulate the formation of new firms in Quebec, provincial legislation provides an exemption for income tax, capital tax, and employer's contributions to the Health Services Fund to certain corporations. This tax exemption applies to active business income, eligible for the small business deduction, during the first five taxation years of new corporations.

A corporation qualifies for the exemption in a taxation year if:

- it is newly incorporated;
- it is not the result of an amalgamation;
- the year is one of its first five taxation years; and
- a tax return is filed within six months after the end of its first taxation year.

A corporation is not eligible for the exemption for the year if, among other things, it:

- was associated with any other corporation;
- was not a "Canadian-controlled private corporation";
- carried on a personal services business; or
- carried on an eligible business as a member of a partnership.

Research and Development. To encourage research and development (R&D) in Quebec, provincial legislation provides several refundable tax credits to certain corporations that carry out R&D in the province.

The basic credit is 20 per cent of wages paid in Quebec for R&D activities in Quebec. If a corporation meets certain criteria and if the expenses are incurred pursuant to particular activities, the rate is increased to 40 per cent on the first $2 million of wages paid in Quebec for corporations whose assets are less than $25 million, and to 40 per cent of all R&D expenses incurred in Quebec pursuant to:

- a university research contract with a prescribed public research centre;

- a pre-competitive research project;
- a catalyst project recognized by the government and certified by the Technological Development Fund, with the possibility of obtaining grants equal to 50 per cent of other eligible expenditures;
- an environmental technology innovation project that has received Technological Development Fund certification (with the possibility of grants equal to 40, 50, or 100 per cent of other eligible expenditures); or
- an R&D consortium project.

The 40 per cent rate on the first $2 million of wages is progressively reduced to 20 per cent, on a linear basis, for corporations whose assets are more than $25 million and less than $50 million.

CHAPTER TWENTY

Facts and Figures for Calculating 1998 Taxes

PROVINCIAL RATES OF TAX FOR 1998 (%)[1]

Alberta	44.0[2, 3, 4]
British Columbia	50.5[3, 5]
Manitoba	51.0[2, 3, 6]
New Brunswick	61.0[3, 7]
Newfoundland	69.0[13]
Northwest Territories	45.0
Nova Scotia	57.5[2, 3, 8]
Ontario	42.75[2, 3, 9]
Prince Edward Island	59.5[3, 10]
Saskatchewan	49.0[2, 3, 11]
Yukon	50.0[3, 12]
Non-residents	52.0

Notes

[1] Rates are expressed as a percentage of basic federal tax. The rates are those in effect at the date of publication.

[2] There are tax reductions for lower levels of income in several provinces, including Alberta, Nova Scotia, Manitoba, Ontario, and Saskatchewan.

[3] Surtaxes and flat tax not included.

[4] Alberta levies a 0.5% flat tax on taxable income and an 8% surtax (not applicable on flat tax) on Alberta tax in excess of $3,500.

[5] British Columbia imposes a 30% surtax on provincial tax in excess of $5,300 and an additional 26% surtax on provincial tax in excess of $8,660.

[6] In Manitoba, a 2% flat tax is calculated on net income. As well, a 2% surtax is calculated on net income in excess of $30,000.

[7] An 8% surtax applies to New Brunswick tax in excess of $13,500.

[8] Nova Scotia imposes a 10% surtax on provincial tax in excess of $10,000.

[9] The Ontario surtax (the "Fair Share Health Care Levy") is 20% on Ontario tax in excess of $4,057.50, plus 33% on Ontario tax in excess of $5,217.50.

[10] Prince Edward Island imposes a 10% surtax on provincial tax in excess of $5,200.

[11] Saskatchewan levies a 2% flat rate tax on net income. A 15% surtax applies to Saskatchewan tax (including the flat tax) in excess of $4,000. An additional 10% surtax applies to Saskatchewan basic tax plus the flat tax. A $150 surtax reduction applies.

[12] Yukon levies a 5% surtax on Yukon tax in excess of $6,000.

[13] Newfoundland imposes a 10% surtax on provincial income tax in excess of $7,900.

FEDERAL RATES OF TAX FOR 1998[1]

Taxable Income	Tax	On Next
$0	$0 + 17%	$29,590
29,590	5,030 + 26%	29,590
59,180	12,724 + 29%	Excess

Note

[1] Table does not incorporate the basic federal surtax of 3% nor the additional 5% surtax on federal tax in excess of $12,500.

FEDERAL RATES OF TAX FOR 1998 INCLUDING SURTAX[1]

Taxable Income	Tax	On Next
$0	$0 + 17.51%	$29,590
29,590	4,051 + 26.78%	29,590
59,180	11,975 + 29.87%	3,015
62,195[2]	12,876 + 31.32%	Excess

Notes

[1] The 3% surtax is reduced in 1998 by a maximum of $125. This reduction is not reflected in the table above. The maximum reduction will rise to $250 in 1999, eliminating the 3% surtax for individuals with income up to about $50,000 and reducing it on a sliding scale for individuals with incomes between about $50,000 and $65,000.

[2] The basic personal tax credit has been taken into account in determining the point at which the high-income surtax begins to apply since, unlike the basic rates (which are applied to taxable income), the surtax applies on tax. The credit has been deducted in calculating the amount of tax.

QUEBEC PERSONAL INCOME TAX MEASURES

1998 Federal Tax—Quebec Only[1]

Taxable Income	Tax	On Next
$0	$0 + 14.71%	$29,590
29,590	3,402 + 22.49%	29,590
59,180	10,057 + 25.09%	3,015
62,195[2]	10,813 + 26.54%	Excess

Notes

[1] The rates take into account the federal surtaxes of 3% and 5% and the 16.5% federal tax abatement for residents of Quebec.

[2] The basic personal tax credit has been taken into account in determining the point at which the high-income surtax begins to apply since, unlike the basic rates (which are applied to taxable income), the surtax applies on tax. The credit has been deducted in calculating the amount of tax.

1998 Quebec Provincial Tax

As of January 1, 1998, the number of income tax brackets has been reduced from five to three. The 5% surtax, the additional 5% surtax and the 2% income tax reduction are incorporated in the new rates. A contribution of 0.3% to the Anti-Poverty Fund applies. The highest marginal rate is reduced from 26.48% to 26.08%. The new tax table is as follows:

Income Tax Bracket	Marginal Tax Rate
$0 – $25,000	20.06%
$25,000 – $50,000	23.07%
Over $50,000	26.08%

1998 Quebec Personal Tax Credits

	Quebec Credit	Federal Tax Credit[1]
Basic	$1,357	$950
Person living alone [2]	242	0
Spouse [3]	1,357	791
Dependent children [4,5]		
first child	598	0
each additional child	552	0
attending post-secondary school [6]— credit per term (max. 2 per year)	380	0
Single-parent family [5,7]	299	0
Other dependants [5,8]		
general	552	0
mentally or physically infirm	1,357	346
Age exemption [9]	506	512
Mentally or physically infirm [10]	506	623

	Quebec Credit	Federal Tax Credit[1]
Pension income [11]	230	147
Member of a religious order	911	0
Lump-sum amount [12]	541	0

Notes

[1] Federal credits for Quebec residents are calculated for a taxpayer at the 17% bracket on the assumption that the credit reduces the federal surtax (3%). The credit also reflects the 16.5% federal abatement.

[2] The credit for an individual living alone is allowed to a single person who maintains a self-contained domestic establishment, or if married, who lives alone or with dependent children. The equivalent-to-spouse credit, which still exists for federal tax purposes, has been replaced in the Quebec system by a combination of the credits for the head of a single-parent family, the credit for the first dependent child, and the credit for a person living alone in a dwelling. Quebec also provides tax reductions for families in addition to these credits, eligibility for which is based on an income test.

[3] In Quebec, this credit is reduced by 23% of the spouse's net income. The word "spouse" includes a common-law spouse. The federal tax credit is reduced by 17% of the spouse's net income exceeding $538.

[4] Dependent children include children, grandchildren, sisters, brothers, nieces and nephews, under age 19 at the end of the year or over 18 and studying full-time.

[5] For all Quebec credits claimed in respect of a dependant or a spouse, the income amount (i.e., the amount before the 23% factor is applied) is reduced dollar for dollar by the dependant's or spouse's net income. Where the additional credits are claimed (e.g., post-secondary studies in addition to basic dependant claim or spouse credit plus transfer of credit for age 65 or over from a spouse), net income is deducted only once from the combined amounts.

[6] This additional credit is allowed when a dependant is in full-time attendance in a post-secondary educational program.

[7] The credit for a single-parent family is available in respect of the first dependent child if the spouse credit is not claimed and the taxpayer does not live with a common-law spouse, is unmarried, or if married, does not live with the spouse and is neither supported by nor supports that spouse. This credit may be claimed for one dependant only.

[8] Other dependants include anyone over 18 years of age who is related to the taxpayer by blood, marriage, or adoption.

[9] In 1998, the federal age tax credit is reduced by 15% of the taxpayer's net income exceeding $25,921. The Quebec tax system has not been harmonized with this federal measure. In certain circumstances, the age credit for taxpayers 65 and over may be transferred from a spouse. In this case, the transferred credit is not subject to the new reduction rules.

[10] The disability credit may also be transferred in certain circumstances to a spouse and other dependants.

[11] Eligible pension income differs for persons age 65 and over, as compared to those under age 65. CPP/QPP benefits and OAS or GIS payments do not qualify, regardless of the taxpayer's age.

[12] Beginning in 1998, individuals are able to choose to use a simplified taxation system that replaces many of the credits and deductions mentioned above by a lump-sum non-refundable tax credit of $541, or 23% of $2,350. This credit can be transferred between spouses if both choose the new simplified system and if the credit cannot be used to reduce the other spouse's tax liability. The more important credits and deductions replaced by the lump-sum credit are contributions to the QPP and employment insurance premiums, tuition fees, support payments made, tax shelters, union or professional dues, medical expenses, taxable capital gains exemption, and transfers to an RPP, RRSP, and RRIF.

Other Quebec Credits and Deductions

Quebec pension plan and unemployment insurance contributions: 23% of contributions, up to specified limits.

Charitable donations: 23% of donations, not exceeding 20% of net income.

Health Services Fund contributions: 23% of contributions, not exceeding $230.

The Quebec tax credit for medical expenses is 23% (17% for federal tax purposes) in excess of 3% of combined net income of both spouses.

For adults respecting the housing of a parent: a refundable tax credit of $550.

COMBINED FEDERAL/PROVINCIAL PERSONAL INCOME TAX RATES FOR 1998[1]

	Alberta			British Columbia			Manitoba		
	Taxes Payable	Marginal Rate on		Taxes Payable	Marginal Rate on		Taxes Payable	Marginal Rate on	
Taxable Income	Other Income	Other Income	Dividend	Other Income	Other Income	Dividend	Other Income	Other Income	Dividend
6,000	0	11.2%	7.4%	0	16.8%	7.0%	0	11.3%	9.6%
8,000	223	18.4%	7.4%	336	26.1%	7.0%	227	30.2%	9.6%
10,000	591	29.5%	7.4%	858	26.1%	7.0%	830	30.2%	9.6%
12,000	1,182	29.5%	7.4%	1,380	26.1%	7.0%	1,434	30.2%	9.6%
14,000	1,772	29.5%	7.4%	1,901	26.1%	7.0%	2,038	30.2%	9.6%
16,000	2,363	27.3%	7.4%	2,423	26.1%	7.0%	2,641	30.2%	9.6%
18,000	2,908	25.3%	7.4%	2,945	26.0%	7.0%	3,245	30.0%	9.6%
20,000	3,415	25.0%	7.4%	3,465	25.6%	7.0%	3,846	29.2%	9.6%
22,000	3,914	25.0%	7.4%	3,976	25.6%	7.0%	4,429	27.7%	9.6%
24,000	4,414	25.0%	7.4%	4,488	25.6%	7.0%	4,983	27.7%	9.6%
26,000	4,914	25.0%	7.4%	5,000	25.6%	7.0%	5,536	27.7%	9.6%
28,000	5,413	27.6%	7.4%	5,511	28.3%	7.0%	6,090	30.4%	9.6%
30,000	5,966	38.5%	23.9%	6,078	39.7%	24.3%	6,698	44.8%	26.9%
32,000	6,736	38.7%	23.9%	6,872	39.9%	24.3%	7,575	44.0%	29.4%
34,000	7,511	38.7%	23.9%	7,671	39.9%	24.3%	8,456	44.0%	29.4%
36,000	8,285	38.7%	23.9%	8,469	39.9%	24.3%	9,337	44.0%	29.4%
38,000	9,059	38.7%	23.9%	9,267	39.9%	24.3%	10,218	44.0%	29.4%
40,000	9,834	38.7%	23.9%	10,065	39.9%	24.3%	11,098	44.0%	29.4%
42,000	10,608	38.7%	23.9%	10,863	39.9%	24.3%	11,979	44.0%	29.4%
44,000	11,383	39.1%	23.9%	11,662	39.9%	24.3%	12,860	44.0%	29.4%
46,000	12,166	40.2%	24.5%	12,460	40.5%	24.3%	13,741	44.6%	29.4%
48,000	12,970	40.4%	24.5%	13,270	40.7%	24.3%	14,633	44.8%	29.4%
50,000	13,778	40.4%	24.5%	14,083	40.7%	24.3%	15,530	44.8%	29.4%
52,000	14,586	40.4%	24.5%	14,897	40.7%	24.3%	16,426	44.8%	29.4%
54,000	15,395	40.4%	24.5%	15,711	43.0%	24.3%	17,322	44.8%	29.4%
56,000	16,203	40.4%	24.5%	16,571	44.6%	26.7%	18,219	44.8%	29.4%
58,000	17,011	42.3%	24.5%	17,463	46.8%	26.7%	19,115	46.8%	29.4%
60,000	17,858	45.0%	30.1%	18,399	49.8%	33.0%	20,051	49.5%	35.2%
62,000	18,759	45.5%	30.1%	19,395	50.3%	33.0%	21,042	50.1%	35.2%
64,000	19,670	45.6%	31.1%	20,401	50.4%	34.0%	22,043	50.1%	36.1%
66,000	20,582	45.6%	31.1%	21,408	50.4%	34.0%	23,045	50.1%	36.1%
68,000	21,494	45.6%	31.1%	22,415	50.4%	34.0%	24,047	50.1%	36.1%
70,000	22,406	45.6%	31.1%	23,422	50.4%	34.0%	25,049	50.1%	36.1%
72,000	23,318	45.6%	31.1%	24,430	50.4%	34.0%	26,052	50.1%	36.1%
74,000	24,230	45.6%	31.1%	25,437	50.4%	34.0%	27,054	50.1%	36.1%

| | Alberta | | | British Columbia | | | Manitoba | | |
| | Taxes Payable | Marginal Rate on | | Taxes Payable | Marginal Rate on | | Taxes Payable | Marginal Rate on | |
Taxable Income	Other Income	Other Income	Dividend	Other Income	Other Income	Dividend	Other Income	Other Income	Dividend
76,000	25,142	45.6%	31.1%	26,444	50.4%	34.0%	28,056	50.1%	36.1%
78,000	26,054	45.6%	31.1%	27,451	53.7%	34.0%	29,058	50.1%	36.1%
80,000	26,966	45.6%	31.1%	28,526	54.2%	36.6%	30,060	50.1%	36.1%
82,000	27,878	45.6%	31.1%	29,609	54.2%	36.6%	31,063	50.1%	36.1%
84,000	28,790	45.6%	31.1%	30,692	54.2%	36.6%	32,065	50.1%	36.1%
86,000	29,702	45.6%	31.1%	31,776	54.2%	36.6%	33,067	50.1%	36.1%
88,000	30,614	45.6%	31.1%	32,859	54.2%	36.6%	34,069	50.1%	36.1%
90,000	31,526	45.6%	31.1%	33,942	54.2%	36.6%	35,071	50.1%	36.1%
92,000	32,438	45.6%	31.1%	35,026	54.2%	36.6%	36,074	50.1%	36.1%
94,000	33,350	45.6%	31.1%	36,109	54.2%	36.6%	37,076	50.1%	36.1%
96,000	34,262	45.6%	31.1%	37,192	54.2%	36.6%	38,078	50.1%	36.1%
98,000	35,174	45.6%	31.1%	38,276	54.2%	36.6%	39,080	50.1%	36.1%
100,000	36,086	45.6%	31.1%	39,359	54.2%	36.6%	40,082	50.1%	36.1%

| | New Brunswick | | | Newfoundland | | | Northwest Territories | | |
| | Taxes Payable | Marginal Rate on | | Taxes Payable | Marginal Rate on | | Taxes Payable | Marginal Rate on | |
Taxable Income	Other Income	Other Income	Dividend	Other Income	Other Income	Dividend	Other Income	Other Income	Dividend
6,000	0	18.0%	7.5%	0	18.8%	7.9%	0	16.2%	6.8%
8,000	359	27.9%	7.5%	377	29.3%	7.9%	323	25.1%	6.8%
10,000	917	27.9%	7.5%	963	29.3%	7.9%	826	25.1%	6.8%
12,000	1,476	27.9%	7.5%	1,549	29.3%	7.9%	1,329	25.1%	6.8%
14,000	2,034	27.9%	7.5%	2,135	29.3%	7.9%	1,832	25.1%	6.8%
16,000	2,593	27.9%	7.5%	2,721	29.3%	7.9%	2,335	25.1%	6.8%
18,000	3,151	27.8%	7.5%	3,307	29.1%	7.9%	2,838	25.0%	6.8%
20,000	3,706	27.4%	7.5%	3,890	28.7%	7.9%	3,338	24.7%	6.8%
22,000	4,254	27.4%	7.5%	4,465	28.7%	7.9%	3,831	24.7%	6.8%
24,000	4,801	27.4%	7.5%	5,040	28.7%	7.9%	4,324	24.7%	6.8%
26,000	5,348	27.4%	7.5%	5,614	28.7%	7.9%	4,817	24.7%	6.8%
28,000	5,896	30.3%	7.5%	6,189	31.8%	7.9%	5,310	27.3%	6.8%
30,000	6,502	42.4%	26.0%	6,825	44.5%	27.2%	5,856	38.3%	23.4%
32,000	7,351	42.6%	26.0%	7,716	44.7%	27.2%	6,622	38.5%	23.4%
34,000	8,204	42.6%	26.0%	8,610	44.7%	27.2%	7,391	38.5%	23.4%

| Taxable Income | New Brunswick | | | Newfoundland | | | Northwest Territories | | |
| | Taxes Payable | Marginal Rate on | | Taxes Payable | Marginal Rate on | | Taxes Payable | Marginal Rate on | |
	Other Income	Other Income	Dividend	Other Income	Other Income	Dividend	Other Income	Other Income	Dividend
36,000	9,057	42.6%	26.0%	9,505	44.7%	27.2%	8,161	38.5%	23.4%
38,000	9,910	42.6%	26.0%	10,399	44.7%	27.2%	8,931	38.5%	23.4%
40,000	10,762	42.6%	26.0%	11,293	44.7%	27.2%	9,700	38.5%	23.4%
42,000	11,615	42.6%	26.0%	12,188	44.7%	27.2%	10,470	38.5%	23.4%
44,000	12,468	42.6%	26.0%	13,082	44.7%	27.2%	11,239	38.5%	23.4%
46,000	13,321	43.2%	26.0%	13,977	45.3%	27.2%	12,009	39.1%	23.4%
48,000	14,185	43.4%	26.0%	14,883	45.5%	27.2%	12,790	39.3%	23.4%
50,000	15,053	43.4%	26.0%	15,793	45.5%	27.2%	13,575	39.3%	23.4%
52,000	15,922	43.4%	26.0%	16,703	45.5%	27.2%	14,360	39.3%	23.4%
54,000	16,790	43.4%	26.0%	17,613	45.5%	27.2%	15,146	39.3%	23.4%
56,000	17,659	43.4%	26.0%	18,523	45.5%	27.2%	15,931	39.3%	23.4%
58,000	18,527	45.5%	26.0%	19,433	49.1%	27.2%	16,716	41.2%	23.4%
60,000	19,438	48.4%	32.1%	20,415	52.8%	35.0%	17,539	43.8%	29.0%
62,000	20,406	49.0%	32.1%	21,470	53.3%	35.0%	18,415	44.3%	29.0%
64,000	21,385	49.0%	33.1%	22,536	53.3%	36.0%	19,301	44.4%	30.0%
66,000	22,365	49.0%	33.1%	23,602	53.3%	36.0%	20,189	44.4%	30.0%
68,000	23,346	49.0%	33.1%	24,669	53.3%	36.0%	21,076	44.4%	30.0%
70,000	24,326	49.0%	33.1%	25,736	53.3%	36.0%	21,964	44.4%	30.0%
72,000	25,306	49.0%	33.1%	26,802	53.3%	36.0%	22,851	44.4%	30.0%
74,000	26,286	49.0%	33.1%	27,869	53.3%	36.0%	23,738	44.4%	30.0%
76,000	27,266	49.0%	33.1%	28,935	53.3%	36.0%	24,626	44.4%	30.0%
78,000	28,247	49.0%	33.1%	30,002	53.3%	36.0%	25,513	44.4%	30.0%
80,000	29,227	49.0%	33.1%	31,069	53.3%	36.0%	26,401	44.4%	30.0%
82,000	30,207	49.0%	33.1%	32,135	53.3%	36.0%	27,288	44.4%	30.0%
84,000	31,187	49.0%	33.1%	33,202	53.3%	36.0%	28,175	44.4%	30.0%
86,000	32,167	49.0%	33.1%	34,269	53.3%	36.0%	29,063	44.4%	30.0%
88,000	33,148	49.0%	33.1%	35,335	53.3%	36.0%	29,950	44.4%	30.0%
90,000	34,128	49.0%	33.1%	36,402	53.3%	36.0%	30,838	44.4%	30.0%
92,000	35,108	49.0%	33.1%	37,468	53.3%	36.0%	31,725	44.4%	30.0%
94,000	36,088	49.4%	33.1%	38,535	53.3%	36.0%	32,612	44.4%	30.0%
96,000	37,077	50.4%	34.1%	39,602	53.3%	36.0%	33,500	44.4%	30.0%
98,000	38,085	50.4%	34.1%	40,668	53.3%	36.0%	34,387	44.4%	30.0%
100,000	39,094	50.4%	34.1%	41,735	53.3%	36.0%	35,275	44.4%	30.0%

| Taxable Income | Nova Scotia | | | Ontario | | | Prince Edward Island | | |
| | Taxes Payable Other Income | Marginal Rate on | | Taxes Payable Other Income | Marginal Rate on | | Taxes Payable Other Income | Marginal Rate on | |
		Other Income	Dividend		Other Income	Dividend		Other Income	Dividend
6,000	0	11.2%	7.4%	0	11.2%	6.7%	0	17.8%	7.4%
8,000	223	18.7%	7.4%	223	29.5%	6.7%	356	27.7%	7.4%
10,000	598	27.3%	7.4%	813	24.8%	6.7%	909	27.7%	7.4%
12,000	1,144	27.3%	7.4%	1,309	24.8%	6.7%	1,462	27.7%	7.4%
14,000	1,690	29.8%	7.4%	1,804	24.8%	6.7%	2,015	27.7%	7.4%
16,000	2,286	32.3%	7.4%	2,299	24.8%	6.7%	2,568	27.7%	7.4%
18,000	2,932	32.2%	7.4%	2,794	24.6%	6.7%	3,121	27.5%	7.4%
20,000	3,576	29.3%	7.4%	3,286	24.3%	6.7%	3,672	27.1%	7.4%
22,000	4,161	26.8%	7.4%	3,771	24.3%	6.7%	4,214	27.1%	7.4%
24,000	4,697	26.8%	7.4%	4,257	24.3%	6.7%	4,756	27.1%	7.4%
26,000	5,232	26.8%	7.4%	4,742	24.3%	6.7%	5,299	27.1%	7.4%
28,000	5,768	29.7%	7.4%	5,228	26.9%	6.7%	5,841	30.0%	7.4%
30,000	6,361	41.5%	25.4%	5,765	37.7%	23.1%	6,442	42.1%	25.7%
32,000	7,192	41.7%	25.4%	6,519	37.9%	23.1%	7,283	42.2%	25.7%
34,000	8,026	41.7%	25.4%	7,277	37.9%	23.1%	8,128	42.3%	25.7%
36,000	8,861	41.7%	25.4%	8,035	37.9%	23.1%	8,973	42.3%	25.7%
38,000	9,695	41.7%	25.4%	8,793	37.9%	23.1%	9,818	42.3%	25.7%
40,000	10,530	41.7%	25.4%	9,551	37.9%	23.1%	10,663	42.2%	25.7%
42,000	11,365	41.7%	25.4%	10,309	37.9%	23.1%	11,508	42.3%	25.7%
44,000	12,199	41.7%	25.4%	11,067	37.9%	23.1%	12,353	42.3%	25.7%
46,000	13,034	42.3%	25.4%	11,824	38.5%	23.1%	13,198	42.8%	25.7%
48,000	13,880	42.5%	25.4%	12,594	38.7%	23.1%	14,054	44.5%	25.7%
50,000	14,730	42.5%	25.4%	13,367	39.8%	23.1%	14,945	44.6%	26.7%
52,000	15,580	42.5%	25.4%	14,164	40.9%	24.4%	15,836	44.6%	26.7%
54,000	16,431	42.5%	25.4%	14,982	40.9%	25.4%	16,728	44.6%	26.7%
56,000	17,281	42.5%	25.4%	15,800	40.9%	24.4%	17,619	44.6%	26.7%
58,000	18,131	44.6%	25.4%	16,618	42.9%	24.4%	18,511	46.7%	26.7%
60,000	19,022	47.4%	31.4%	17,475	47.3%	30.2%	19,445	49.7%	33.0%
62,000	19,971	47.9%	31.4%	18,421	50.2%	33.0%	20,440	50.2%	33.0%
64,000	20,929	48.0%	32.4%	19,426	50.3%	34.0%	21,445	50.3%	34.0%
66,000	21,889	48.0%	32.4%	20,432	50.3%	34.0%	22,451	50.3%	34.0%
68,000	22,849	48.0%	32.4%	21,437	50.3%	34.0%	23,457	50.3%	34.0%
70,000	23,809	48.0%	32.4%	22,443	50.3%	34.0%	24,463	50.3%	34.0%
72,000	24,769	48.0%	32.4%	23,449	50.3%	34.0%	25,469	50.3%	34.0%
74,000	25,729	48.0%	32.4%	24,455	50.3%	34.0%	26,475	50.3%	34.0%

	Nova Scotia			Ontario			Prince Edward Island		
	Taxes Payable	Marginal Rate on		Taxes Payable	Marginal Rate on		Taxes Payable	Marginal Rate on	
Taxable Income	Other Income	Other Income	Dividend	Other Income	Other Income	Dividend	Other Income	Other Income	Dividend
76,000	26,689	48.0%	32.4%	25,461	50.3%	34.0%	27,481	50.3%	34.0%
78,000	27,649	48.8%	32.4%	26,466	50.3%	34.0%	28,487	50.3%	34.0%
80,000	28,624	49.7%	33.5%	27,472	50.3%	34.0%	29,493	50.3%	34.0%
82,000	29,618	49.7%	33.5%	28,478	50.3%	34.0%	30,499	50.3%	34.0%
84,000	30,611	49.7%	33.5%	29,484	50.3%	34.0%	31,505	50.3%	34.0%
86,000	31,604	49.7%	33.5%	30,489	50.3%	34.0%	32,511	50.3%	34.0%
88,000	32,597	49.7%	33.5%	31,495	50.3%	34.0%	33,517	50.3%	34.0%
90,000	33,591	49.7%	33.5%	32,501	50.3%	34.0%	34,523	50.3%	34.0%
92,000	34,584	49.7%	33.5%	33,507	50.3%	34.0%	35,529	50.3%	34.0%
94,000	35,577	49.7%	33.5%	34,512	50.3%	34.0%	36,535	50.3%	34.0%
96,000	36,570	49.7%	33.5%	35,518	50.3%	34.0%	37,541	50.3%	34.0%
98,000	37,564	49.7%	33.5%	36,524	50.3%	34.0%	38,547	50.3%	34.0%
100,000	38,557	49.7%	33.5%	37,530	50.3%	34.0%	39,553	50.3%	34.0%

	Quebec					Saskatchewan		
	Taxes Payable			Marginal Rate on		Taxes Payable	Marginal Rate on	
Taxable Income	Federal	Quebec	Combined	Other Income	Dividend	Other Income	Other Income	Dividend
6,000	0	0	0	21.5%	17.9%	0	14.6%	9.9%
8,000	186	244	430	34.5%	17.9%	292	27.8%	9.9%
10,000	476	645	1,121	34.5%	17.9%	849	32.8%	9.9%
12,000	765	1,046	1,812	34.5%	17.9%	1,506	32.8%	9.9%
14,000	1,055	1,447	2,502	34.5%	17.9%	2,163	27.8%	9.9%
16,000	1,345	1,849	3,193	34.5%	17.9%	2,719	27.8%	9.9%
18,000	1,634	2,250	3,884	34.5%	17.9%	3,276	27.8%	9.9%
20,000	1,922	2,651	4,573	34.3%	17.9%	3,833	28.4%	9.9%
22,000	2,206	3,052	5,258	34.3%	17.9%	4,400	28.4%	9.9%
24,000	2,490	3,453	5,943	35.8%	17.9%	4,967	28.4%	9.9%
26,000	2,774	3,885	6,658	37.3%	21.6%	5,535	28.4%	9.9%
28,000	3,058	4,346	7,404	38.8%	21.6%	6,102	31.2%	9.9%
30,000	3,372	4,807	8,180	45.4%	31.4%	6,725	42.8%	27.6%
32,000	3,818	5,269	9,087	45.6%	31.4%	7,581	43.0%	27.6%
34,000	4,268	5,730	9,998	45.6%	31.4%	8,441	43.0%	27.6%

		Quebec				Saskatchewan		
		Taxes Payable		**Marginal Rate on**		**Taxes Payable**	**Marginal Rate on**	
Taxable Income	**Federal**	**Quebec**	**Combined**	**Other Income**	**Dividend**	**Other Income**	**Other Income**	**Dividend**
36,000	4,718	6,192	10,909	45.6%	31.4%	9,301	43.0%	27.6%
38,000	5,168	6,653	11,820	45.6%	31.4%	10,161	43.4%	27.6%
40,000	5,617	7,114	12,732	45.6%	31.4%	11,029	45.2%	29.1%
42,000	6,067	7,576	13,643	45.6%	31.4%	11,933	45.2%	29.1%
44,000	6,517	8,037	14,554	45.6%	31.4%	12,837	45.2%	29.1%
46,000	6,967	8,498	15,465	46.1%	31.4%	13,741	45.8%	29.1%
48,000	7,428	8,960	16,388	46.3%	31.4%	14,657	46.0%	29.1%
50,000	7,894	9,421	17,315	49.3%	35.1%	15,577	46.0%	29.1%
52,000	8,359	9,943	18,302	49.3%	35.1%	16,496	46.0%	29.1%
54,000	8,824	10,464	19,289	49.3%	35.1%	17,416	46.0%	29.1%
56,000	9,290	10,986	20,276	49.3%	35.1%	18,366	46.0%	29.1%
58,000	9,755	11,507	21,263	50.5%	35.1%	19,255	48.1%	29.1%
60,000	10,243	12,029	22,272	52.0%	38.4%	20,217	51.0%	35.3%
62,000	10,762	12,551	23,313	52.6%	38.4%	21,237	51.5%	35.3%
64,000	11,292	13,072	24,364	52.6%	39.3%	22,268	51.6%	36.3%
66,000	11,822	13,594	25,416	52.6%	39.3%	23,299	51.6%	36.3%
68,000	12,353	14,115	26,468	52.6%	39.3%	24,331	51.6%	36.3%
70,000	12,884	14,637	27,521	52.6%	39.3%	25,363	51.6%	36.3%
72,000	13,415	15,158	28,573	52.6%	39.3%	26,394	51.6%	36.3%
74,000	13,945	15,680	29,625	52.6%	39.3%	27,426	51.6%	36.3%
76,000	14,476	16,201	30,677	52.6%	39.3%	28,458	51.6%	36.3%
78,000	15,007	16,723	31,730	52.6%	39.3%	29,489	51.6%	36.3%
80,000	15,537	17,245	32,782	52.6%	39.3%	30,521	51.6%	36.3%
82,000	16,068	17,766	33,834	52.6%	39.3%	31,553	51.6%	36.3%
84,000	16,599	18,288	34,886	52.6%	39.3%	32,584	51.6%	36.3%
86,000	17,129	18,809	35,939	52.6%	39.3%	33,616	51.6%	36.3%
88,000	17,660	19,331	36,991	52.6%	39.3%	34,648	51.6%	36.3%
90,000	18,191	19,852	38,043	52.6%	39.3%	35,679	51.6%	36.3%
92,000	18,722	20,374	39,096	52.6%	39.3%	36,711	51.6%	36.3%
94,000	19,252	20,895	40,148	52.6%	39.3%	37,743	51.6%	36.3%
96,000	19,783	21,417	41,200	52.6%	39.3%	38,774	51.6%	36.3%
98,000	20,314	21,939	42,252	52.6%	39.3%	39,806	51.6%	36.3%
100,000	20,844	22,460	43,305	52.6%	39.3%	40,837	51.6%	36.3%

| | | Yukon | | | Non-Resident | |
| | Taxes Payable | Marginal Rate on | | Taxes Payable | Marginal Rate on | |
Taxable Income	Other Income	Other Income	Dividend	Other Income	Other Income	Dividend
6,000	0	16.7%	7.0%	0	17.0%	7.1%
8,000	335	26.0%	7.0%	339	26.4%	7.1%
10,000	855	26.0%	7.0%	866	26.4%	7.1%
12,000	1,375	26.0%	7.0%	1,393	26.4%	7.1%
14,000	1,895	26.0%	7.0%	1,920	26.4%	7.1%
16,000	2,415	26.0%	7.0%	2,448	26.4%	7.1%
18,000	2,936	25.9%	7.0%	2,975	26.2%	7.1%
20,000	3,453	25.5%	7.0%	3,499	25.8%	7.1%
22,000	3,963	25.5%	7.0%	4,016	25.8%	7.1%
24,000	4,473	25.5%	7.0%	4,533	25.8%	7.1%
26,000	4,983	25.5%	7.0%	5,049	25.8%	7.1%
28,000	5,493	28.2%	7.0%	5,566	28.6%	7.1%
30,000	6,058	39.6%	24.2%	6,139	40.1%	24.5%
32,000	6,850	39.8%	24.2%	6,941	40.3%	24.5%
34,000	7,645	39.8%	24.2%	7,747	40.3%	24.5%
36,000	8,441	39.8%	24.2%	8,553	40.3%	24.5%
38,000	9,236	39.8%	24.2%	9,359	40.3%	24.5%
40,000	10,032	39.8%	24.2%	10,165	40.3%	24.5%
42,000	10,828	39.8%	24.2%	10,971	40.3%	24.5%
44,000	11,623	39.8%	24.2%	11,777	40.3%	24.5%
46,000	12,419	40.4%	24.2%	12,583	40.9%	24.5%
48,000	13,226	40.6%	24.2%	13,400	41.1%	24.5%
50,000	14,037	40.6%	24.2%	14,222	41.1%	24.5%
52,000	14,848	40.6%	24.2%	15,044	41.1%	24.5%
54,000	15,660	40.6%	24.2%	15,865	41.1%	24.5%
56,000	16,471	40.6%	24.2%	16,687	41.1%	24.5%
58,000	17,282	42.5%	24.2%	17,508	43.1%	24.5%
60,000	18,133	45.8%	30.0%	18,370	45.8%	30.4%
62,000	19,048	46.5%	30.5%	19,286	46.3%	30.4%
64,000	19,978	46.5%	31.4%	20,213	46.4%	31.3%
66,000	20,909	46.5%	31.4%	21,141	46.4%	31.3%
68,000	21,840	46.5%	31.4%	22,069	46.4%	31.3%
70,000	22,771	46.5%	31.4%	22,997	46.4%	31.3%
72,000	23,702	46.5%	31.4%	23,925	46.4%	31.3%
74,000	24,633	46.5%	31.4%	24,853	46.4%	31.3%

| | Yukon | | | Non-Resident | | |
| | Taxes Payable | Marginal Rate on | | Taxes Payable | Marginal Rate on | |
Taxable Income	Other Income	Other Income	Dividend	Other Income	Other Income	Dividend
76,000	25,564	46.5%	31.4%	25,781	46.4%	31.3%
78,000	26,494	46.5%	31.4%	26,709	46.4%	31.3%
80,000	27,425	46.5%	31.4%	27,637	46.4%	31.3%
82,000	28,356	46.5%	31.4%	28,565	46.4%	31.3%
84,000	29,287	46.5%	31.4%	29,493	46.4%	31.3%
86,000	30,218	46.5%	31.4%	30,421	46.4%	31.3%
88,000	31,149	46.5%	31.4%	31,349	46.4%	31.3%
90,000	32,080	46.5%	31.4%	32,277	46.4%	31.3%
92,000	33,011	46.5%	31.4%	33,205	46.4%	31.3%
94,000	33,942	46.5%	31.4%	34,133	46.4%	31.3%
96,000	34,873	46.5%	31.4%	35,061	46.4%	31.3%
98,000	35,803	46.5%	31.4%	35,989	46.4%	31.3%
100,000	36,734	46.5%	31.4%	36,917	46.4%	31.3%

Note

1. The taxes payable take into account only the federal personal tax credit of $1,098 and the Quebec personal tax credit of $1,357. Marginal rates for capital gains are three-quarters of the rates shown for Other Income.

Index

258 ◄ **Index**

Deloitte & Touche LLP Offices

British Columbia

Langley	(604) 534-7477
New Westminster	(604) 664-6200
Prince George	(250) 564-1111
Vancouver	(604) 669-4466
Victoria	(250) 360-5000

Alberta

Calgary	(403) 267-1700
Edmonton	(403) 421-3611

Saskatchewan

Prince Albert	(306) 763-7411
Regina	(306) 525-1600
Saskatoon	(306) 343-4400

Manitoba

Winnipeg	(204) 942-0051

Ontario

Guelph	(519) 822-2000
Hamilton	(905) 523-6770
Hawkesbury	(613) 632-4178
Kitchener	(519) 576-0880
London	(519) 679-1880
Mississauga	(905) 803-5100
Ottawa	(613) 236-2442
Sarnia	(519) 336-6133
St. Catharines	(905) 688-1841
Toronto	(416) 601-6150
Toronto North	(416) 229-2100
Windsor	(519) 258-8833

Québec
(Samson Bélair/Deloitte & Touche)

Alma	(418) 669-6969
Amos	(819) 732-8273
Baie-Comeau	(418) 589-5761
Chicoutimi	(418) 549-6650
Dolbeau	(418) 276-0133
Farnham	(514) 293-5327
Granby	(514) 372-3347
Grand-Mère	(819) 538-1721
Hull	(819) 770-3221
Jonquière	(418) 542-9523
La Baie (Ville De)	(418) 544-7313
La Malbaie	(418) 665-3965
Laval	(514) 978-3500
Matane	(418) 566-2637
Montréal	(514) 393-7115
Québec	(418) 624-3333
Rimouski	(418) 724-4136
Roberval	(418) 275-2111
Rouyn-Noranda	(819) 762-0958
Saint-Hyacinthe	(514) 774-4000
Sept-Îles	(418) 968-1311
Sherbrooke	(819) 564-0384
St-Félicien	(418) 679-4711
Trois-Rivières	(819) 691-1212

New Brunswick

Fredericton	(506) 458-8105
Moncton	(506) 857-8400
Saint John	(506) 632-1080

Nova Scotia

Halifax	(902) 422-8541

Newfoundland

St. John's	(709) 576-8480

National Offices

Toronto (150 King)	(416) 599-5399
Toronto (95 Wellington)	(416) 601-5650
Siège social du Québec (Montréal)	(514) 393-7115

The Deloitte & Touche Guide to
Retirement Planning

Whether you're a typical Canadian worker, a corporate executive, or a business owner, you will retire someday, but before you do, you need to read this indispensable guide from one of the largest accounting and management consulting firms in Canada. It will help you lay the groundwork for a worry-free future.

Preparing for retirement is complicated and requires very careful planning. Gone are the days of the gold watch and the single small pension. Today we retire with larger incomes from a greater number of sources than ever before. The Deloitte & Touche Guide to Retirement Planning recognizes this, and will help you develop your own personal strategy for a comfortable and worry-free retirement. You will discover 71 easy-to-find RetireTips that highlight key retirement planning strategies for workers, corporate executives and business owners. As well, this user-friendly guide includes information on:

- Government and employer benefits
- Estate and succession planning
- RRSPs and other financial strategies
- Retiring outside Canada
- Sources of income for the business owner
- And much more

Written by the tax-, retirement- and estate-planning experts of Deloitte & Touche, this comprehensive book will give you all the tools you need to begin to make your retirement everything you want it to be.

Available in book stores across Canada. Get your copy today!

$19.95

KEY PORTER BOOKS

Deloitte & Touche

www.deloitte.ca

It's there for you!

Writing books like this is one way we try to help you reach your goals, but it's not the only way!

Our Web site provides another option by offering you instant access to a broad range of information and resources. At the click of a mouse, you can, for example:

- *check out what's new*
- *search for information you need*
- *read our publications*
- *learn about our firm, its expertise and the industries we serve*
- *investigate careers with us*
- *link to related sites around the world*
- *and much more!*

We encourage you to visit the site whenever you have a moment. It's easy to navigate, and we hope you'll find it useful each time you visit. Also, your comments and suggestions are important to us; that's why you can contact us directly from the site.

So drop by soon. We're looking forward to your visit.

70%
of family-owned businesses don't survive their founder's departure ...

How can you help your business beat the odds?
By planning ahead for its success!

At Deloitte & Touche LLP, we've developed a comprehensive planning package to help family-owned businesses beat the odds, survive and prosper.

It's called Continuum -
A Systematic Approach to Success Planning - and it helps you

Save tax dollars now

Build your wealth for the retirement lifestyle you want

Minimize family conflicts over the leadership of your business

rotect your business, your family and yourself should you become disabled

Continuum is designed to give you a comprehensive plan tailored to the specific needs of your business, your family, and you. And your plan isn't just for today. It's a flexible program that adapts to your changing needs and circumstances. As part of the program, we help you take stock of your business and family circumstances, provide you with a professional evaluation of the issues and options you face, work with your other advisors to help implement your action plans, and conduct a regular review to keep your plan up-to-date and effective.

Want to beat those odds? Get Continuum working for you.

Call us today.

CONTINUUM
A systematic approach to success planning

More information is available from any of our offices in Canada, or call John Bowey, our Continuum coordinator, at (519) 576-0880, Email jbowey@deloitte.ca, or Fax (519) 576-0209.